**Investment in education and social choice**

# Investment in education and social choice

TAPAS MAJUMDAR

CAMBRIDGE UNIVERSITY PRESS

*Cambridge*
*London   New York   New Rochelle*
*Melbourne   Sydney*

Published by the Press Syndicate of the University of Cambridge
The Pitt Building, Trumpington Street, Cambridge CB2 1RP
32 East 57th Street, New York, NY 10022, USA
296 Beaconsfield Parade, Middle Park, Melbourne, Australia



First published 1983

Printed in the United States of America

*Library of Congress Cataloging in Publication Data*
Majumdar, Tapas.
Investment in education and social choice.
Bibliography: p.
Includes index.
1. Education – Finance. 2. Education – Economic aspects. 3. Educational equalization. I. Title.
LB2824.M34 1983 338.4'337 82–12829
ISBN 0 521 25143 5

*To* BHABATOSH DATTA
Professor Emeritus, Presidency College, Calcutta,
who invested wisely in human capital
so that his *students* might reap
the returns

# Contents

# Tables

# Preface

This brief study arose out of an attempt to answer the following simple question: What happens to the economics of education when the "market" for education is described in terms of investment in human capital (following Schultz), rather than in terms of demand and supply of a consumption good or service?

In pursuing this question the initial problem one faces is understanding the established paradigms of economics of education, which are all analogues of those that predominate in main-line economics. I have tried to argue that the usual analogies are often discovered in the end to have been far too simplistic, precisely because investment in education requires a more complicated framework for its proper description. This study tries to make explicit the nature of the complications involved and to suggest a more comprehensive structure of analysis. The framework developed in this monograph is based on the interrelationship of three basic concepts one encounters in economics of education. These are categories one must consider if one visualizes a choice situation in terms of investments in human capital and assumes that these investments come into being through conscious decision-making processes.

The first of these concepts concerns what I have suggested is a special feature of investment in education that, in addition to being theoretically interesting, has important policy implications. This is the notion of the aggregate investment in education as being a composite of two different kinds of investments involved in education: investment by some for procuring or buying their education, and investment by others – individuals, institutions, or society – for providing or selling that education. This implies the combination of two different though complementary categories of investment decisions. To combine them and thereby treat investment in education the same as one would, for example, investment in a steel mill (where the two-part distinction does not exist) is an unsatisfactory and theoretically unwarranted extension of the physical capital analogy to economics of education.

The second concept is that of the well-known micro–macro distinction in economic analysis. In the context of investments in education the notion emerges naturally because decision makers in the individual domain and those in the institutional or societal domain are different sets of agents. Microeconomic considerations alone are relevant for the former. But macroeconomic considerations pertaining to the economy as a whole and the implications of the microeconomic considerations of individual decision makers both must be considered by societal investors in education. Thus this notion again implies an essentially two-part division of simultaneous and sometimes conflicting micro–macro considerations in educational investments. This division, I have felt, has sometimes been glossed over in the analysis of social policy with respect to investment in education.

The third notion that emerges is one that obviously is not at all specific to the economics of education. That is, in fact, the fundamental notion of social choice as *collective* choice, and it would apply to the analysis of economic policy in general. Regrettably, it has not yet become common practice in discussions of economic policy to combine the positive macroeconomic argument with the welfare-economic considerations of the underlying social-choice questions. And yet, these considerations come to the fore as soon as the question of interpersonal comparability of any kind is raised, or the question of deciding which set of collective-choice rules should hold is discussed. A combination of macroeconomic and social-choice considerations, strangely enough, has been even rarer in discussions on investment in education. But surely it is here that the composite character of the economic argument should be seen as even *more* crucial, because here we have to make judgments on investments embodied in, and specific to, persons in contrast to the relatively impersonal investments in nonhuman capital of the conventional type.

Three different, though related, arguments are developed in this study that correspond to the three basic concepts. I have called these the domain-distinction argument, the micro–macro argument, and the collective-choice argument, respectively. The framework of the study is as follows. Chapter 1 discusses the general applicability of the usual paradigms of main-line economics to education and concludes with a plea for analysis in terms of more heterogeneous structures in the economics of education. Such heterogeneity would seem to be fully justified by the existing state of research in the field though it is not yet embodied in the standard textbooks. Chapter 2 elaborates on the three basic theoretical arguments of this monograph that I have already mentioned. Chapter 3 attempts a critique – not quite original by itself but formulated in terms of these arguments – of the conventional approaches to measuring rates of return to investment in education in terms of omnibus and homogenized categories such as number of years of formal education. Most of the criticisms here are well known, and I have attempted to place these and similar criticisms in the context of the three basic arguments, which is the only novel feature.

Chapter 4 is devoted to a somewhat more positive application of theory to the discussion of selected examples that are largely hypothetical though based on actual case studies from several countries. Here my purpose is to bring out the interpersonally differentiated character of the returns to individual investments in education and the consequent dilemmas in choice involved in interpreting the returns from society's point of view for arriving at optimal investment decisions. Chapter 5 concludes the analysis by attempting to classify the various types of social-choice dilemmas discovered in the examples discussed in Chapter 4. Here I have attempted briefly to consider in the light of the foregoing analysis the basic complexity of the relationship between considerations of equity and efficiency in educational investments.

I have tried to keep the treatment both within the bounds of theoretical economics and accessible to readers in the general field of education, in the belief that the subject deserves to be examined in depth by workers in more than one discipline. I must confess, however, to having been quite uncomfortably conscious of the risks entailed in trying to talk simultaneously to people in two different disciplines, particularly when, as in this case, the proffered scheme of analysis is meant largely to be tentative and not definitive.

I am happy to express my sincere gratitude to the following, without whose active support this study would not have been possible:

The authorities of the Institute of Development Studies (IDS) at the University of Sussex, England, for the invitation to spend a year at the institute. The intellectual interests pursued at the institute, spanning several disciplines and many countries, provided a highly congenial atmosphere for the type of study I was interested in and the study profited thereby in many ways.

The authorities of Jawaharlal Nehru University, New Delhi, for granting me leave of absence from the university's Zakir Husain Centre for Educational Studies in the School of Social Sciences.

John Oxenham for initiating and sponsoring my stay at the IDS; for unflinchingly reading more than one draft of the manuscript; and for showing me the noneconomist's side of the argument on most questions and, I hope, most of the time.

Amartya Sen for reading and extensively commenting on the drafts.

Shrawan Kejariwal and Prasanta Pattanaik for reading parts of the manuscript and making valuable comments.

Charles Cooper and Ronald Dore for their kind and active participation in my preliminary seminar on the subject and for many subsequent conversations at the IDS.

Louis Levy-Garboua of the University of Paris-I for the long and helpful discussions of the book at the Centre de Recherche pour l'Etude et l'Observation des Conditions de Vie, Paris.

Michael Debeauvais for arranging a seminar on the theme of this monograph at the International Institute for Educational Planning in Paris and for providing in subsequent conversation several valuable insights.

Binod Khadria and N. V. Varghese for reviewing the final typescript and for providing a number of extensive comments and many references.

Maureen Dickson and J. S. Baweja for invaluable secretarial assistance.

Finally, to be completely truthful, I must confess somewhat shamefacedly, but happily, that I could not possibly have finished this monograph on time if my wife Gauri had not consented to keep a strict and watchful eye on its progress and helped with the planning of the study and, above all, if our daughter Srinayana had not gladly approved of the arrangement.

None of the aforementioned, I need hardly add, can be held responsible for the errors and omissions that remain in the monograph.

TAPAS MAJUMDAR

CHAPTER 1

# Analogies of economics for economics of education

## 1.1 The range

If one considers Schultz's 1960 study to be its genesis, the economics of education can be said to have barely come of age. It is still largely a new and unexplored area, but at least two propositions, first formulated in Schultz's classic contribution, can be said to have been reasonably well established – notwithstanding a number of ideological and semantic quibbles. The first proposition is that the outcome of a process of learning is a new form of productive resource: *human capital*.[1] A second proposition, obviously related to this, is that the decision to spend scarce resources on education is an *investment* decision precisely in the sense in which the term would be understood in plain economics.[2] To date the birth of these two propositions from Schultz's 1960 work is not to say, as Blaug (1968 p. 11) rightly observed, "that nobody published in this field or even that nobody used the label 'economics of education' before 1960, but simply that most economists before 1960 were not aware of the fact that widely different observed economic phenomena could be rendered intelligible by the idea of human capital formation."[3]

The two related ideas of learning as human capital formation and, consequently, of spending on education as investment will play an important part in this study. I shall argue, however, for restraint in making the usual analogies between physical capital formation and human capital formation and investment in education.

Although the basic soundness of Schultz's two propositions cannot be questioned, the same could not be said of a third proposition that also has been of great theoretical and econometric interest. This proposition states that education is a process of simple production (e.g., Woodhall and Blaug, 1965, 1968). This analogy is, as I will show, deceptive as well as grossly inadequate. It obscures more than it enlightens a process that by all accounts has remained largely intractable, despite many attempts to unravel its mysteries.

Obviously, economists analyzing activity in a new area for the first time will not automatically begin by looking for new first principles or by trying out their latest ideas. Rather, they are on the lookout for, and wisely so, theoretical and analytical constructs that already belong to their standard repertoire and happen to appear promising at the beginning of the analysis. They try to fit some of these constructs into plausibly analogous situations encountered in the new area of study. That economists for the most part have done precisely this over the last twenty years in the field of education, and on a fairly formidable scale, is therefore, by itself, not a particularly remarkable feature of the development of the economics of education. What may be remarkable, however, is that many analogies of main-line economics occasionally seem to have been forcibly transported into education even when they obviously traveled rather poorly. Even where the limitations and objections to the analogies were well understood, they have been used. The broad and compelling purpose of economics of education seems to have been to describe the processes in education as *normal* economic activities. This obviously oversimplified, rather than clarified, the picture that economists really sought to draw. Economists themselves have frequently pointed out what may be called an obscurantist role of oversimplifications in the analysis of economic processes in education, and I refer to some of the well-known instances in Section 1.5. But the practice certainly survives in the standard textbooks of economics of education.

### *Three types*

It would be useful to look at the analogues of "normal" economics that have been brought to the economics of education. I cite three different types that correspond respectively to the three propositions – different but not unrelated – discussed in the preceding section.

The first proposition, it may be recalled, is based on Schultz's concept of human capital and it provides a counterpart to the notion of physical capital formation. I shall discuss the extent of the admissibility of the physical capital analogue in education in Section 1.2.

The second set of analogies centers around the proposition that spending resources on education is an act of investment. The analogies here are in terms of the choice situation present in investment in human capital. The analogues would thus be (a) the investment decision makers in education, corresponding to investors in the capital market; (b) the alternative opportunities in education, corresponding to alternative investment channels in the normal economy; and (c) the "choice rule" to be used in investment decisions in education, corresponding to the typical returns-maximization rule of the normal capital market.

Finally, the third set of analogies appears to illustrate the proposition that the activity of education can best be characterized as a normal process of production carried out by the firm. The analogy that is usually presented in economics of education at this level (Woodhall and Blaug, 1965, 1968) is between modern industrial production in a factory and the educational process organized in a formal structure. This analogy is examined in Section 1.4.

The point I wish to make is that the two propositions about human capital and investments in human capital formation are useful only as starting points of analysis. The essential peculiarity and specificity of individual human capital, the heterogeneity of individual and group purposes and the division and interrelation of their respective domains for investments in education, the resulting conflicts and dilemmas for macroeconomic decisions in such investments, and, above all, social-choice questions as questions essentially of *collective* choice – all these must be elaborated carefully in the subsequent steps.

As to the third proposition, the implication of any essential similarity in terms of structure between the processes of education and normal economic processes will be shown to be false and highly misleading. In fact, the structural similarities, even such as do exist, quickly disappear once we move outside the formal systems of education. For example, it is true that the school and the factory have far too many *formal* similarities for the analogy between them to be considered farfetched at first sight. But even a quick probe will invariably show the comparison to be almost totally unsatisfactory, as I shall show. Moreover, when it comes to the more general case of the not necessarily formal processes of education, economists find even less use (and excuse) for the analogies. Economists, for one historical reason or another, were concerned first with the resource allocation problem arising in the formal systems of education. This in turn provided them with analogues, almost fortuitously, of a number of familiar variables of normal economic analysis. One can only speculate as to how economics of education would have developed had economists started with the problems of nonformal education.

I shall now deal further with my general point about the analogies by running quicky through a short list of the "proxies" that one finds extensively in economics of education – proxies that correspond to the more familiar variables that had primarily been validated in economics in the first place. Though these are arranged to correspond to the three propositions, the three sets of analogies need not be seen as mutually exclusive.

## 1.2 Human capital

As Schultz recognized:

> Although it is obvious that people acquire useful skills and knowledge, it is not obvious that skills and knowledge are a form of capital, that this capital is in substantial part a product of deliberate investment, that it has grown in Western societies at a much faster rate than conventional (nonhuman) capital, and that its growth may well be the most distinctive feature of the economic system. It has been widely observed that increases in national output have been large compared with the increases of land, manhours, and physical reproducible capital. Investment in human capital is, probably, the major explanation for the difference.[4]

Schultz then proposed that investment in education be looked upon as a major form of investment in human capital. Ever since, the great analogy between investment in education and investment in physical capital has continued. Many studies have appeared attempting to measure in specific situations the marginal efficiency of this very special kind of investment and have established it as a new species of investment made for economic returns as in all other sectors of the economy.[5] The returns from investment in education, following the analogy, become comparable to returns from investment in physical capital for the allocation of resources by investment decision makers.

### *Some peculiarities: a contrariness*

Placing human capital formation in the more general context of investment analysis as known to normal economics is an extremely fruitful exercise. But in the course of that exercise, several special features of human capital formed through education may be lost or pushed to the background. These features, however, deserve to be noted, for they may well represent a basic difference between the two kinds of capital: that embodied in a machine and that of an educated mind.[6]

In the first place, a machine will necessarily wear out and depreciate not merely with the passage of time but with use (and will depreciate more with more intensive use). In other words, a machine must work subject to the normal constraints of economic costs if it works at all. The educated mind, on the other hand, can behave quite contrarily because it can, in favorable circumstances, enrich itself merely through continued use. That is, human capital, unlike a piece of machinery, is sensitive to how it is being used and what it is being used for. It can be enhanced or replenished if used in one way, but will only wear itself out and get stale in another setting.[7] A recording of a teaching program is worn out to a degree often measurable in terms of the number of hours it is played. The human lecturer, on the other hand, may well become more valuable human capital merely by teaching the same number of hours as the recording was played. This contrary nature of human capital is often overlooked by economists and educational technologists alike.

It is well known that programs of nonformal education can often contrive and maintain conditions under which the enhancement of the human capital used would be the rule rather than the exception. It is equally well-recognized that the rigidity of formal teaching systems would make that the exceptional experience of only a handful of gifted teachers in ordinary situations or particularly fortunate teachers in highly congenial working conditions. Economists of education cannot easily operationalize the implication of this two-way quality of human capital for the evaluation or planning of education as an activity, because although human capital *can* behave anti-mechanically, it does not necessarily do so. It seldom does so, for example, in a modern impersonal teaching shop. If the reaction of human capital in different working conditions could be estimated, there would be an obvious implication also for the estimation of human capital costs.

The supply price of a teaching activity insofar as it is based on the teacher's perception either of the old disutility of labor or of the rate of depreciation of human capital (whichever way it is stated) can therefore take two extreme values (and probably many intermediate ones). The actual value would depend, of course, on what the teaching activity in question is expected to do to teachers. If they are merely being worn out, like machinery, then their cost is full, let us say, 1. If they are being replenished or, in fact, enriched by the teaching experience, then their cost is zero. This essentially binary character of human costs is bound to play an important role in the determination of the costs of many educational activities.

For example, economists have sometimes noted that the dominant and an increasing proportion of costs in all nonformal education projects today is for items other than human.[8] One reason for this could be that among other characteristics, nonformal programs seem much more able to draw on dedicated voluntary service than does the formal education system. It would be wrong, however, to attribute this characteristic mainly to the spirit of service among the teachers involved, or alternatively, to the quick ability of the organizers of nonformal programs to cash in on that spirit. If economists could manage to bring out the 0–1 range characteristics of human capital costs in a given program of educational activity, then they could at the same time learn to represent genuine alternative human cost options in the program. This task would not be helped by a straightforward analogy between human and physical capital.

### *Returns as resource or benefit*

The possible self-enrichment through use of human capital and the resultant characteristics of human capital costs would no doubt justify a certain measure of optimism in the estimate of expected costs in a process of education when it is planned specifically to take advantage of this possibility. It is necessary, however, to set the balance right by pointing out a second factor that operates in the opposite direction. The social profitability of investment in education is, on the whole, an *imputed* profitability and is not based on the generation of resources or a transferable surplus, at least in the short run.

There are two reasons why a high expectation of the generation of benefits and a comparatively low expectation of the costs of education do not by themselves imply that the surplus can be generated as a resource to be recycled for the sustenance or expansion of a given educational activity. The first reason is the known relative preponderance of external productivity in almost any worthwhile basic (or primary) educational activity. The larger part of the surplus generated by investment in education is outside and not within the source of the primary activity, which is quite unlike profit (even social profit) generated through investments in physical capital by the activity of a normal economic enterprise. Profit, in normal investment, arises largely as private profit within the enterprise and can only marginally spill over through the externalities. Therefore, in the case of educational investments, except possibly those in the sector of higher education, it would be extremely difficult, if not impossible, even adequately to trace back to the decision makers the major part of the social benefits they actually generate.

Similarly, barring a complicated, uncertain, and arbitrary set of imputations, it would be equally difficult to devise a system of taxation and bounties that could repay the investment decision makers responsible for an educational activity for the surplus they helped create. This, in fact, also gives rise to the second reason why some investment activities in education might be given no social subsidy for their externalities, even if one knew precisely how much they were worth to society, when producing a set of illiquid assets. Put simply, taxing the external beneficiaries on gains that they could not readily turn into cash would be practically impossible in the short run even if a satisfactory method of counting the benefits could be devised. Higher levels of health, a better quality of life, even the assurance of increased productivity in the long run are valuable economic assets. But they lack the one important quality of monetary resources: liquidity. They cannot be sold or exchanged at will to assure the viability of a project.

Thus, economists of education must accept it as their lot, more so than other welfare economists, that they may have to commend a given project on grounds of real economic returns, while pointing out that there are insufficient prospects of the economic resources' being generated for maintaining or replicating the same project. This paradox is, of course, not totally unknown in normal economics, particularly in the appraisal of investments that generate high externalities in the form of nontransferable assets. But for the economics of education this is indeed a basic feature that enthusiasts of many new high-yielding varieties (in real terms) of investment in education overlook in their great hurry to begin a project, only to be eventually surprised by the drying up of resources before it ends.

*Domains of decision making*

I shall conclude this section by briefly introducing another absolutely basic feature of human capital formation – one, moreover, that this study largely concerns. This feature stems from the fact that human capital formed through the process of education depends on investments made in two complementary parts and decided in two domains.[9] Students can invest their time and money in their own education in a particular field only if somebody else, an institution or, perhaps, society as a whole, also invests in providing them with that education. In turn, the institutional or societal investment can be meaningful only if there are students who will invest their own time and money to get that education. Investment in nonhuman capital generally does not show this two-domain characteristic that I shall elaborate further in my discussion of the domain-distinction argument in Chapter 2.[10]

Even without elaboration, one can see that the simple distinctions between the two kinds of conditions existing for decision making in the formation of human and physical capital, respectively, would make the usefulness of pursuing the analogy between the two extremely dubious. Indeed, one might argue that, to the extent that the analogy focused only on the similarity and blurred the distinctions, it played a partly obscurantist role in the analysis. For example, the inability to distinguish clearly and at all times between the characteristics and purposes of institutional education-providing investments and individual education-seeking investments would certainly seem too high a price to pay for the sake of the analogy. The deficiency of a "unified" definition of aggregate investment in education would be serious enough even if the object were to judge only the market consequences of investment policy from a positive-economic point of view. From a welfare-economic standpoint, the deficiency would be disastrous.

## 1.3 Education as investment

The purpose of using the analogy of investment in physical capital, or investment in the capital market, to describe the choice situation in education is obviously to establish for the "investor" in education a logic of investment decisions that can relate such decisions to investment opportunities in the economy as a whole. The rate-of-return approach in economics of education has sought to provide precisely that logic. Here the analogy shifts from the relatively difficult characterization of capital itself to the operationally more manageable level of the investor as the decision maker. The choice is represented in this context as analogous to that prevailing for investments in physical capital where investors base their choices on comparisons of the different expected marginal rates of return.

There can be no quarrel with the basic proposition that investments in education are to be viewed as deliberate, optimizing decisions. But, as I shall elaborate in Chapter 3, there are two difficulties with this simple analogy with normal investments. In the first place, the alternatives available in educational investment cannot easily be placed in the same category as alternative investment opportunities in the usual sense. For one thing, investments in education are generally one-shot: A student cannot stay back in primary education and spend more time on it after seeing that secondary education is less remunerative, for example. For another, investments in education are generally structured sequentially: Students cannot skip secondary education and go for their doctorates because this happens to be more rewarding. Such difficulties with the interpretation of the rates of return to education have been noted by many, and I shall also refer to some of them in Chapter 3.

The second difficulty with the analogy stems from the problem of pinning down the investor in education. The two domains of investment in education – the individual and the institutional or societal – have two sets of investors who have two different sets of objectives, time horizons, and purposes. A rate-of-return approach that obscures some of this essential distinction between the choice situation in the normal capital market and that in education thus necessarily remains inadequate.

Many of the difficulties that a straight analogy between investment in education and investment in physical capital is likely to encounter have already been discussed individually in the literature of economics of education. But I shall argue that these, too, are best handled in the general framework of the three arguments I have sought to distinguish in my treatment. These arguments are based on (a) the separate treatment of domains of investment in the way I have already mentioned; (b) the separate roles visualized in investment decision in education for micro–macro judgments; and (c) the recognition that all social-choice questions in investment in education are really questions of collective choice.[11] The arguments will be introduced in Section 1.5 and their theoretical basis dealt with in detail in Chapter 2.[12]

## 1.4 Education as production

Let me turn now to a third type of analogy that has been brought into economics of education: the production–function analogy.

The most obvious analogy between a process of production in the economy and a formal educational process is in terms of comparison of structures. The paradigm that has been brought into economics of education for this purpose is typically that of a modern industrial plant in which raw materials enter at one point, and finished outputs exit at subsequent points, a sequence of net values being added between the points.[13] This sequence and its usual organization in the factory system appear to be simulated in the system of formal schooling based on a comparable hierarchical structure. Here, too, the raw material (beginning with the 5-year-olds) enters the conveyor belt of an educational process that moves on as additional inputs such as teachers, books, and equipment are applied, and the net value is added to the product stage after stage. The analogy identifies the students as raw material, the necessary inputs, the graduates as the output, the directed sequence itself as the production process and, above all, the firm as the decision maker. It is, therefore, also accepted as a matter of course that the process is so described as to conform to the well-known maxim for the firm: Given costs, maximize output (or, given output, minimize costs) – costs and outputs being, of course, the categories identified as such in the analogy. Let me first refer in this connection to two interesting examples in the literature of how far the analogy has been carried in characterizing education as a productive process and the lessons to be derived from such characterization on the lines of the conventional theory of the firm.

First, take the quantitative aspect of productivity itself, which, despite many obvious difficulties in definition, has always been a highly regarded indicator of efficiency in normal economics. It is not surprising, therefore, that economists would sooner or later seek to conceptualize productivity of an educational process analogously in economics of education in their legitimate search for an efficiency criterion. Woodhall and Blaug (1965, 1968), for example, used the formal and structural similarities between the factory and the school precisely for this purpose. They tried to obtain measures for educational productivity in British universities for the period 1938–62, and in secondary schools for 1950–63. "We do not imply a rigid analogy between the university and the factory: We will in fact examine some of the ways in which the process of education differs from that of manufacturing. We are convinced, however, that the comparison as such is illuminating."[14] When it comes to identifying the output, they admit, "in the present analysis we must perforce limit ourselves to what can be readily quantified and measured. In the case of higher education the end-product is simply a degree."[15]

Second, consider the question of the optimum size of the firm. Jenny (1968) discusses the optimum size of a university as a non–profit-making firm treating the question in light of the other, more familiar question in the theory of the firm: that of the optimum size of the profit-making firm.

Clearly, whether it is a question of productivity or the optimum size of the educational institution, the analogy of the firm requires definition of the output, the costs of production, the principle of optimization given relative input and output prices, and, above all, the decision maker or the firm. I shall try to recapitulate some of the well-known problems with the production analogy by taking the analogous definitions in the same order.

### *The well-defined output*

Possibly the least controversial aspect of a normal economic enterprise is the definition of its output. Many problems are often encountered in measuring the quality or even the quantity of the output of a modern firm, particularly if it is a multiproduct firm. There is seldom any difficulty, however, in identifying its principal outputs without ambiguity. But, as Woodhall and Blaug (1965) observe:

> The first problem in considering the education industry is to define output. What is the end-product of a period of schooling? One of the peculiar features of universities is that they represent a vast multiproduct industry, providing teaching and research in a wide range of subjects at many different levels. All these elements have to be combined and expressed in equivalent units. Furthermore, the final product is intangible, and at first sight, incapable of being quantified. When physical measures are not avail-

able, as in the case of all service industries, the common procedure is to use money values adjusted by a price index as an estimate of quantity. But there is no market mechanism for universities and so no money valuation of output.[16]

This is intended to be the justification for treating the end product as "simply a degree." The formal system of education can indeed be shown, in this sense, to have a structural similarity to industrial production. If one takes the number of diploma holders emerging from an educational process as the output of that process, then the analogy is close enough; a possible difference is that no industrial process would normally survive the proportion of rejects that a formal educational system often accepts not only as usual, but actually as an indicator of its high standard of production.[17]

It may not be possible, however, to justify taking the number of diploma holders as output merely because it can be "readily quantified and measured." It is well accepted that neither the purpose nor the outcome of a process of education can be as easily and incontrovertibly defined as in an industrial process. In fact, depending on what one accepts as the main societal purpose of a given system of education, the number of diploma holders may only sometimes be a reasonable indicator of achievement; at other times, with the prospect of unemployment, for example, it is a rather poor indicator. The output of a larger number of barely educated graduates when the felt societal need was for a smaller number of properly educated ones would be another case in point. Again, as economists of nonformal education would point out, in some not necessarily formal process of education the intended output itself may well be so diffuse or else so external to the process as to render it practically undefinable as a working analogue or proxy for *output* as understood within a normal economic process.

### *The unit cost of production*

Unit costs are intended to be used as efficiency indicators. The inverse of unit costs would be an index of total-factor productivity in a production process, which is defined as output per unit of all the inputs combined. Provided the implicit index-number problem in fixing the relative weights for making up a composite unit of inputs is recognized, this would also be a useful index of efficiency in a process in which individual contributions of the inputs need not or cannot be separated.

The usual proxy for the unit cost in the field of educational economics is the cost of education per student. It is no longer unusual to come across studies of average cost curves for individual educational institutions or for alternative courses of study for purposes of comparison. The extent of implied relative subsidies to students in different streams is often estimated or debated on this basis. Yet, the theoretical justification for using costs calculated per student as the relevant unit cost of education has never been very clear. Even if the number of students is accepted as a reasonable measure of the output desired in the first place, an additional assumption is needed to make cost per student yield an operationally meaningful index of efficiency of production for optimization. It would be necessary to assume that the defined output and the costs can be varied so that the optimizing principle of maximization of output, given costs, can be worked out in the process of production. As long as the output of the educational process cannot be fully specified as an increasing function of costs incurred in education so that it is assumed that quality remains unchanged with changes in unit costs (as in the case of industrial production), the use of cost per student as a general index of efficiency will be generally fallacious.[18] The similarity of the educational institution to the firm, therefore, will break down when pressed to the point of making such an assumption.

Even as an index of only the internal efficiency of the process, cost per student may be wide of the mark because of an additional feature that sharply distinguishes an educational process from an industrial one. For want of a better name, I shall call it the *group effect* on the quality of education. To produce five good sports cars, to take an example from manufacturing high-quality products in a normal economic enterprise, it should not be necessary to produce them in a larger group with fifteen other cars for company and encouragement. But to produce five good physicists it may well be necessary to put them in a class of twenty. This is so not only because students have a tendency to try to keep up with and improve upon one another, but also because they can often learn from one another rather than from the appointed teacher and the other planned inputs.

There may be another factor that usually does not attract our attention: Education itself is essentially a groping and probing process. It may act like the filter that Arrow (1973) postulated separates the good from the indifferent, but perhaps it may do so only after long and continuous search. It is only at the end of the day that it will be discovered which five, among twenty of equal promise, blossom into the high-powered physicists that society had intended to produce. I do not attempt to go beyond the statistical and probabilistic explanation of this phenomenon. Perhaps the real explanation lies in the different abilities of equally gifted individuals to benefit from the external effects of the other individuals in the group.[19] Even so, it may be in the nature of things that the process of discovering this differential is inseparable from the process of education. Whatever the explanation, if the educational situation is such that the quality attained by some is known to depend on competition or even on inclusion in a larger group, or if the high-quality output is expected to emerge only probabilistically as part of a larger output of the process, then we must beware of the analogue of unit cost. The cost-per-student approach to efficiency calculation then would lose its validity almost entirely.

I need only to add by way of digression that, first, the external productivity of the education process is generally admitted to be even more predominant in nonformal than in formal systems. Second, the aforementioned externality effect on the quality of the product or the effect of the group on the individual is likely to be more manifest within groups engaged in educational activities demanding high social motivation and interaction than within groups of students only doing formal course work. The cost of education per student, a construct of uncertain usefulness even within purely formal systems, is therefore even more uncertain for the more general case of not necessarily formal structures of educational processes.

### *Optimum-input coefficients*

Production possibility curves are usually assumed to be continuous over the factor space. Given strict convexity and a set of prices for the factors of production, this implies a unique set of input coefficients that will be the optimum set for a given output. In other words, if relative factor prices remain unchanged, a given output is associated with inputs joined in fixed quantities. Assuming constant returns to scale all around, this will imply fixed input ratios whatever the output. This assumption is frequently used for all kinds of standard projections of inputs and outputs, and provided one knows the limitation of the assumption, it can be useful.

The translation of the optimum-input coefficient to the field of education, however, has proved to be quite a different matter. The student–teacher–books–buildings ratio enjoys a greater sanctity in the bureaucracy of educational planning than main-line economists had ever intended for the points on the production possibility curve that are revealed as the optimum points under the appropriate relative input prices. This is presumably because the coefficients often regarded as ideal by educational planners are not the outcomes of the relative-prices situation at all but of some implicit, and possibly unfounded, "technological" consideration in education.[20] But, of course, an analogy resting more on administrative usage than on sound economics cannot be improved merely through the use of sound technique or by a determined pursuit of the illusive educational production function.

Recalling the preceding discussion on the well-defined output and the unit cost of production in the education "industry," one would be inclined to suspect the usefulness of the production function analogy itself in education. Moreover, the problem of choosing the optimum input mix in an educational process must be formulated with reference to the question of who will choose the optimum or the most cost-effective mix. It is here that the analogy begins to disintegrate completely because *within* the input mix is visualized one input, namely, students, who are the decision makers in their own domain of investment in education.

### *Raw material as decision maker?*

Finally, we are confronted by the most incongruous aspect of the analogy between the factory and the school. "One problem of applying a productivity index to universities," Woodhall and Blaug (1965) stated, "is that the student is both an input and an output of the system. Our measure of output is in fact an estimate of the 'value added' by the process."[21] A far greater problem, however, they left unmentioned: Students are also investment decision makers in their own domain, in addition to being both *inputs* and *outputs* of the system. And as I have pointed out, and will elaborate in Chapter 2, side by side with that individual domain of students who buy their education is the complementary domain of investment for providing that education.

Who, then, is the decision-making firm in the system?[22] Is it the individual who is also the primary raw material? Is it society or the institution that invests in the school? Are they, perhaps, jointly the decision-making firm? These questions, of course, are merely rhetorical. The truth is that the analogy between the firm and the school has broken down completely at this point.

## 1.5 A plea for a new economics of education

The constraints that the economics of education operates under and the fallacies it encounters certainly lead one to question the appropriateness of the paradigms applied to it from main-line economics. But the difficulty is not so much with the imported ideas as with their associated structures. The present study may, indeed, be understood to be a plea for a New Economics of Education. But it should not be seen as a plea for abandoning any of the following themes: (a) the concept of human capital itself; (b) the presentation of the process of learning as a conscious optimization process; and (c) the idea that the organization of education produced a recognizable outcome or output even though what was being produced could be subject to both uncertainty and controversy. These are the themes that underlie the three propositions concerning the formation of human capital, education as investment, and education as production. As I have suggested, the difficulty with their treatment in economics of education has not been with the basic themes as such, but rather with the often simplistic paradigms that put the underlying ideas in straitjackets. Specifically, the difficulty has been with the assumptions of homogeneity – whether of the structures of investment in education, of the domain and category of decision makers in educational investments, or of the class of the beneficiaries of the decisions.

The plea, therefore, is for other paradigms on the same themes and essentially for a reexamination of structures that often have been already seen by economists of education to be heterogeneous even if not universally treated as such. The heterogeneity in the structures, for example, of human capital itself or of the process of decision making or of the set of decision makers in education, has been discussed in individual instances by many workers. For example, Ben-Porath (1967) notes that some kinds of human capital might just as well improve as other kinds deteriorate with use – a point elaborated on in Section 1.2. Schultz (1967) speaks of different time horizons of investment decisions in education that are implicit in the rates of return tables and the actual investment behaviors of the individuals and schools – a point that has appeared in more elaborate form in terms of the domain-distinction argument developed in this study. Rosen (1972) suggests a model of sequential learning options exercised by individuals through contracts in the job market itself, which, by implication, builds on the essentially sequential character, to be discussed in Section 3.5, of all investment in education. Johnson and Stafford (1973) find different, higher marginal rates of return to education with respect to expenditure on quality, rather than years of schooling, which clearly brings out one of the limitations of the conventional calculation of the rate of returns that I shall speak of. Frances Stewart (1975) points out the consequences of conflicting group interests and preferences for the measurement of social costs and benefits of an investment project, thus raising the basic social-choice problem at the heart of this study.[23]

Thus, few of the criticisms that I make of the homogeneity assumptions of conventional economics of education can, by themselves, lay claim to any particular novelty. I have tried, on the contrary, to incorporate in the structure of analysis what should be seen mainly as elaborations of the basic themes of economics of education along three lines. These elaborations are prompted by the class of these and similar other possible criticisms that could have been made, whether or not they are actually recorded in the literature.

The first line of elaboration is to spell out the nature of heterogeneity in the structure of investment decisions in education. What I have called the domain-distinction argument is based on the notion that investment in education for any purpose has essentially two parts: one part in the domain of the learner, the other in institutional, societal hands. In other words, investment to receive education and investment to provide education are visualized as two separate, complementary, and not always matching components of what is otherwise described as simply *the* investment in education.

A second line of elaboration with a similar theme is developed under what I call the micro–macro argument. This is used to describe the heterogeneity of investment decisions from yet another angle contrasting investment decisions of individuals based on legitimate microeconomic logic with the institutional or societal investment decisions that often must take into account the microeconomic considerations of individuals and aggregate macroeconomic considerations.

Recognition of the heterogeneous structure of investment decision making in education leads this study in the direction of a third, final line of elaboration. This, it is suggested, concerns the collective-choice questions involved in consideration of the juxtaposition or the aggregation of conflicting and competing individual interests and judgments for arriving at societal judgments on investment decisions in education. I have called this the collective-choice argument.

I plead, therefore, for an understanding of the heterogeneity of investment decisions, first, in terms of the distinction of the two domains in investment in education, and second, in terms of the contrast and interplay of micro- and macroeconomic considerations. Finally, and above all, I plead for an understanding of the social-choice dilemmas that inevitably surface as soon as it is recognized that society's judgments on investment decisions in education must be represented basically as collective judgments and that social choice must be represented as collective choice. It is in the incorporation of these three arguments, which I elaborate on in Chapter 2, that I would suggest the future of the new economics of education must lie.

CHAPTER 2

# Investment decisions in education

## 2.1 Decision making in education

Perhaps the most noticeable aspect of the structure of investment decisions in education is its own special kind of heterogeneity. This structural heterogeneity sharply distinguishes investment in education from other kinds of investment decisions. I shall argue that the failure to recognize this as a basic characteristic of educational investments has often resulted in the application of some of the simplistic analogies noted in the preceding chapter.

One of the aspects of heterogeneity that I shall try to develop in the course of this study as a prominent feature, and one that occupies most of my treatment here in any case, would perhaps deserve special mention. It is, simply, the distinction between investments made by or on behalf of individuals for procuring or buying their education, and all investments made (whether by individuals or institutions) for providing them with that education. It may be recalled that I referred to this basic feature in concluding Section 1.2.

Another interesting feature of this heterogeneity is the existence of several types of interdependence, seen from either the individual or the economy-wide point of view, that are known to hold between different available channels of investment opportunities. I shall try to show that the macroeconomic consequences of the aggregate of investment decisions in education become clearer when these two distinguishing features are taken into account in more explicit terms than normally allowed. The problem of social choice in education also emerges in sharper focus and the question of measuring the social return to education can be better related to the state of aggregate unemployment, to inequality of opportunities, and to general questions of equity when these features of heterogeneity are taken into account.

I shall begin by bringing in individual and societal decision makers in Sections 2.2 and 2.3, respectively. By individual investment decisions I shall mean decisions taken by individuals for *buying* their own or their dependents' education, that is, education-seeking investment decisions. All investment decisions toward providing education for individuals, whether by individuals, private or public institutions, or the state, I call, admittedly somewhat inaccurately, institutional decisions. These decisions regarding education-providing investments presumably would be subject to societal judgment or even control in one form or another.

## 2.2 Investment in education: individual decisions

The first point to make about the heterogeneity of the structure of individual investment decisions in education is that the returns, however defined, would be singularly unsuitable for analyzing the logic of individuals' allocation of resources between successive levels of their own schooling. One compelling reason inhibiting between-levels comparability of returns from the individual standpoint is as follows. Increments of schooling at different levels of education do not belong to the same set of alternatives before individuals when they have to invest in their own schooling at any point in time. If, as a primary school graduate, I am considering buying high school education for myself, then the knowledge, let us say, that primary education currently presents prospects of rather lower returns than I can now expect of high school education tells me nothing whatsoever about how I should allocate my available resources. I obviously cannot allocate less funds (or indeed more) to my own past. Moreover, it is interesting that even if I could consider the two levels together (such as when I pay for other people's education, as will be discussed) the *quantum* of investment required for a year's schooling in the formal system varies so widely between different levels of education that the comparison still might not be meaningful for me if I have only limited command of resources.

The other aspect of the sequential nature of investment in formal schooling would be clear if one remembered that just as I cannot consider my past investment opportunities in education as alternatives because they are past, I also cannot consider future opportunities as alternatives if they are contingent on the present. The prospect of a higher return to postgraduate education at the university level, for example, cannot possibly induce me to withhold resources from my perhaps less profitable high school education (in fact, it can have quite the opposite effect), because high school is a necessary step to university.

It would follow that if I am observed to have gone successively into each level of education, then the additional fact that the marginal rates of return, if calculated for the different levels, are (or are not) observed to be equal is entirely fortuitous. It does not imply that I have been able (or unable) to achieve optimum allocation of resources between the levels. In other words, the marginal rates of return to investment at the various levels of schooling (assuming that they can be, and have been, properly estimated) can have no comparability between themselves from the standpoint of individuals investing in their own education, because their admission into successive levels cannot be alternative opportunities for them at any point in decision making.

In one sense, however, the comparability between investment opportunities at different levels of schooling can be preserved from the standpoint of individual decisions, in the special case of decision makers' being assumed to be concerned not only with their own schooling prospects but also with the prospect of educating other family members. For example, some parents might conceivably consider choosing between (a) financing all their children up to an identical level of schooling, and (b) financing some of the children further than the others, keeping in view the returns to investment for the family as a whole. I have already mentioned one reason why it might not be useful to compare the returns between levels of schooling that would hold even in this case. It is simply that the minimum investments required by the system for the two levels concerned might be too widely disparate.

For example, if an Indian family must spend around Rs. 100 a year for the primary education of one child but around Rs. 1,000 a year for the higher education of another child, then two opposite considerations may weigh with the decision maker at the same time. On the one hand, a higher *rate* of return from *primary* education might be less attractive if the *total* returns are considered important: Rs. 50 per year from higher education rather than Rs. 8 per year from primary education, for example, with no other alternative investment opportunities. On the other hand, a higher rate of return from higher education might look more attractive but the capital cost of Rs. 1,000 a year might be way out of the family's reach given the imperfections of the capital market.

We shall see in Chapter 3 in some detail how, in two distinct ways, the conventional rate-of-return approach in economics of education has usually limited itself. In the first place it has rarely considered the problem of comparability, that is, whether the given investment opportunities are really alternatives for the individual decision maker. Second, it has generally disregarded the importance of counting *all* investment opportunities in education rather than only the opportunities for lengthening the period of schooling. Obviously, a full economic analysis of the alternative investment decisions in education faced by individuals must consider their *complete* alternatives set of opportunities. I shall try to set out what such a complete set of alternatives is likely to consist of. This should also bring out a distinction that I will need to make later between measuring the marginal returns to education corresponding to increments in the length of schooling and the marginal returns to education corresponding to increments in investment.

If I had additional resources to spare for buying more of all things, including education, then I could think of several alternative ways of spending it – if I found it worthwhile to spend it at all. For example, I could (a) set it aside, as assumed in the conventional approach, for continuing beyond the present level of schooling, going out for a higher-level certificate. I could equally (b) choose a costlier, but hopefully, more rewarding course.[1] Or I could (c) go to a more expensive and better school. I could even (d) devote more time to my studies, thereby forgoing some income, but expecting to acquire a higher degree of proficiency in a future income-earning activity. For the same reason, I could (e) buy more expensive books and equipment. I might also (f) find some feasible combination of some or all of these five alternatives as *the* alternative of my choice. Finally, I might (g) opt out of the formal system of education altogether, finding it more profitable to acquire a skill through a system of nonformal or continuing education, in service or even out of service.

Let us presume that individual investors in education seek only economic returns. One way in which they then can be described as maximizing their expected net returns would be in terms of improvements in their own lifetime earnings. But obviously, the highest return on their outlay calculated in terms of earnings need not necessarily come from spending another year in schooling. To anticipate an argument that comes up in the next chapter, a rate-of-return table that advises them of returns from adding to the level of education in terms of number of years of schooling only obviously will not necessarily inform them about the best option at any given point in decision making. Indeed, it might turn out to be more rewarding to go for better (or more) education *at* a level, than to invest funds for only average education *beyond* that level. Therefore, even for individual family investors, who can compare between levels of education when they seek to invest for maximum returns, the rate of return to increments in schooling does not provide the kind of information that the rate of return to physical capital provides for making investment decisions in capital markets elsewhere in the economy.

Let me now conclude this section by setting down two propositions that have emerged in the preceding discussion on the logic of individual investment decisions in education.

*Proposition 1: Levels of schooling are not real alternatives for individual choice.* Investments at different levels of education that must be made in a sequence over time are not real alternatives for individuals investing in their own education, at any given point in decision making.

*Proposition 2: There are other alternatives.* The rate of return to investment in education that should be of real concern to individuals at any point in decision making is the highest marginal rate of return they can expect from among *all* alternative investment opportunities open to them, only *one* of these being the opportunity to extend the length of schooling to reach the next higher level.

## 2.3 Investment in education: institutional decisions

It may be recalled that the distinction between institutional and individual decisions in investment in education, in our definition, is that the former identifies those decisions made, by whichever agents, for providing (or selling) education, and the latter denotes those made by or for individuals for procuring (or buying) their education. This simple distinction, though straightforward enough, is still liable to be overlooked by economists because they persist in thinking in terms of the analogy of investment opportunities in a conventional capital market.

The distinction between investments made toward providing a service and investments made toward obtaining it emerges naturally in education. In other areas of investment this particular distinction generally does not exist. It is true that the paradigm of a homogeneous category of investor also creates some problems for the treatment of investment decisions involving physical capital. Particularly when the basis of the decisions is represented as social returns to investment, and especially if a corresponding homogeneity is not assumed in society itself, the questions of interpersonal comparability and equity, and collective-choice considerations in general, make the paradigm difficult to sustain. But still, collective-choice problems are rarely a central issue in the economics of societal investment decisions. Moreover, the complexity in investments in education would arise also because the dichotomy between individual and institutional investors is an additional factor to consider over and above the usual distinction welfare economics makes between the social and the private costs and benefits of every type of investment.

An immediate implication of the distinction between the two types of investment decisions in education is that a given rate of return to investment will not necessarily mean the same thing for both. In fact, casual observation would suggest that even the main categories of expenditure on which institutional investments in education are concentrated would in general be very different from those that attract individual investments – for example, outlays on school buildings and teachers' salaries in the former case and tuition and income forgone in the latter. The implications of the distinction between the two kinds of decisions, however, are far from casual. Three different levels of consideration appear to be associated with the distinction, and all three must be brought together for an adequate analysis of investment decisions in education. I shall briefly introduce the three levels of argument here, developing them somewhat more fully in Sections 2.4, 2.5, and 2.6.

The first and most obvious set of considerations that would arise following the distinction between individual and institutional investment decisions constitutes what I shall call the *domain-distinction argument*. By *domain* I mean precisely the category of investments in real terms that a given class of decision makers can consider. For example, if I act as an individual decision maker in education, then the objects in which I can consider investing my resources to buy education belong to the individual domain. On the other hand, if I act as an institutional decision maker, then the objects for which I can allocate resources to provide education to other individuals will belong to the institutional domain.

Although the two kinds of investments in the two domains have to be, in some ways, complementary, not only their physical characteristics but also their respective purposes can be very different. For one thing, the time horizon against which one must judge, from the standpoint of society, most types of institutional investment in education would be necessarily much wider than that against which individuals are presumed to make their investments with their own lifetime returns in view. These considerations would, of course, be quite specific for each case and would suggest to what extent and in what sense a proposed investment in education could be expected to satisfy the different ends pursued in the two domains.

A second set of considerations constitutes what I shall call the *microeconomic–macroeconomic argument* or, for brevity, the micro–macro argument.[2] These are the quantitative considerations resting on the size of investments in education in the aggregate. The societal judgment would have to take into account two kinds of quantitative considerations at the macroeconomic level. The first concerns the possible impact of a particular investment activity on the market as a whole, determined by the size of that activity. Since the usually contemplated size of an institutional investment activity is much larger than the outlay the individuals themselves can consider in their domain, a large institutional investor in education cannot hope to rely on the ruling market prices' remaining stable with the same confidence as the individual investor perhaps can.

A second kind of consideration then would also follow from the same logic. If societal judgment must consider possible changes in the market situation due to the size of investments, then surely it must take into account not only the size of a contemplated institutional or societal investment but also its total impact on the market in terms of the aggregate of all anticipated investments, including investments in the individual domain that are likely to accompany it. On either of the considerations the macroeconomic argument would caution the societal investor against trusting that a set of ruling prices and rates of factor earnings in the market would remain dependable parameters for making investment decisions. Thus, one task before the societal decision maker would be to separate the macroeconomic from the microeconomic arguments for investment decisions in the market.

The third and final set of considerations, whether in making societal investment decisions or in assessing *all* investment decisions from a societal point of view, constitutes the *collective-choice argument*.

In an important sense this is the culmination of the arguments at the other two levels of domain-distinction and macro–micro dilemmas. In fact, the main point about the arguments at the other levels is that they can, in principle, and often do in practice, lead to contradictory social-choice positions, as I shall try to show. This is because in education, as in other areas of the economy, the individual interests to be served are many and conflicting; moreover, individual judgments of what is in society's interest also widely differ.[3] Thus implicit in the social valuation of *all* investments in education, whether they be in the individual or the institutional domain, are considerations of interpersonal comparability and aggregation of welfare.

This is the crux of the collective-choice argument. At the risk of oversimplifying, I should describe its purpose as mainly to expose, and not necessarily resolve, the contradictions inherent in the social-choice situation. As applied to societal judgment on investment decisions in education, the argument encourages one to ask not only (a) what should be counted as the social returns to education, but also (b) whose perception would help to determine what would count as the social returns to education, and (c) how, that is, through what process of aggregation, the social returns would be tallied. These are difficult questions to answer for all investments, particularly social investments. But they are especially difficult for investments in education because here, besides other complications, including domain distinction, it is always possible that the real beneficiaries of a particular societal investment are often heavily outnumbered by the rest of society, who are nevertheless made to pay for it.

I shall follow up this general introduction to the three levels of societal concern in investments in education by elaborating each separately. But let me do so after first introducing a hypothetical example. It is a somewhat complicated one, but it covers quite a simple and familiar situation in educational decision making, at least in many Third World economies. At the risk of being repetitive, I will have occasion to come back to this example a number of times. Suppose society must decide whether to provide further training for a number of science graduates that would enable them to take a course for a specified period (for example, a year) at the end of which successful graduates earn an additional degree (bachelor's degree in technology).

One of the first questions to ask in this case, from the standpoint of societal decision makers, is what individual decision makers think of this opportunity. Therefore, let me take the individual domain first. Professionally trained science graduates, let us assume, are known to have a high (say, 90%) probability of securing the relatively better paid position of a trained science graduate, on the completion of their technical degree. They are also known to have, let us assume, a high probability (say, 90%) of completing their technical course successfully. Would-be trainees, who seek to assess their prospects in terms of probable improvements in their lifetime cost–income stream can try to estimate their personal rate of return by going through the following steps, though not necessarily in the same order. First, they could try to determine the expected returns corresponding to the technical degree level in the labor market. Second, they would assess the probability of their being able to complete the technical courses successfully – they may or may not accept the average probability, known to be 90%. Third, they would note the probability, also known to be 90% in this case, of getting the higher paid job on having completed the course successfully. Fourth, they would then adjust *downward* their original rate of return figure, which was based on the certainty of successes, by taking into account the two values of the probability of failures they would have noted in the preceding two steps. Finally, they would adjust this figure up *or* down depending on their own degree of confidence and risk-proneness.

The logic of institutional investment decisions, from society's point of view, in providing that technical course, however, will have to run along more complex circuits. Individual decisions in their own domain will have to be anticipated, but society will also have to consider its own reasons. To forestall one confusion that may be caused by my definitions, I should stress here that the institutional decisions are not necessarily to be assumed to be made on societal considerations. It may well be that our particular institutional investor – a private school, for example – provides the facilities for education from a standpoint other than that of society as a whole. Such investors may even be acting on the basis of their own private motives. But, if only for simplicity of presentation, the treatment here is restricted to the point of view of the whole society to assess institutional investment decisions, whatever the motives underlying them.

## 2.4 The domain-distinction argument: complementarity of domains and variety of time horizons

The operational significance of the domain-distinction argument is that although institutional investment can provide the educational or training facilities, only individuals' efforts and investments will make it possible for them to take advantage of them.[4] Unless the two kinds of investments match there can be only empty, or overcrowded, classrooms and under- or oversubscribed training programs. This, then, is the first, or at least an early, consideration of the domain-distinction argument applied to a particular choice situation. No matter what the social benefit from a particular mode of institutional investment is assessed to be, the first operationally important question for the institutional investor is: Will it sell? It may be said that the conventional human labor planning approach to investment in education tends to overlook this question altogether. The conventional rate-of-return approach, in turn, makes the mistake of postulating a single category of investors, failing to distinguish between the two complementary domains of investment in education. The proposition that decisions in the institutional domain are made by one set of agents who may not have quite the same objectives as, but who have to rely on the individual domain decisions made by, another set of agents (and vice versa) provides what I shall call the "complementarity-of-domains aspect" of the argument.

A second, and what I shall call the "time-horizon" aspect of the domain-distinction argument arises if we consider the wide variety of the lengths of lifetimes one has to take into account, explicitly or implicitly, when one assesses the costs and benefits of investments in education.[5] The important distinctions here are of two types. First, one can, of course, divide the life-span considerations for investments in education broadly between the two domains. All the individual investment decisions, then, would fall on one side, and many of the societal investment decisions on the other. Second, one can distinguish the longer-term from the short-term considerations within the domain of institutional investment itself.

With regard to the first distinction, it would be sufficient to point out that societal investments, in many significant cases, will have much longer life spans to consider than individuals' investments.[6] Individuals, after all, have only their own lifetimes – or the lifetime of whomever they are investing for – to consider when estimating relevant cost–income streams. But societal judgment on institutional investment in education often has to consider the impact of an investment decision on not one, but several generations of people. Even the physical characteristics of the investments in question in either category (buildings in one, exercise books in the other, say), to no one's surprise, tend to match the longer or the shorter time horizon in view.

One interesting upshot of the domain-distinction argument at this point, therefore, is simply this: A market signal of returns to education, if judged to have only short-term stability, would be less useful for making a societal judgment on providing a line of education than for taking the individual decisions to go and invest on *securing* it. I should point out, however, that if this is an adverse verdict against institutional investments, particularly of the long-term kind, in the presence of uncertainty as to how long the present prospects will hold, it has nothing to do with the problems of identification and measurement of the social costs and benefits of education. The uncertainty involved here is the temporal uncertainty of the market, and not the vagueness associated with the definition and perception of social costs or benefits of education.

The second distinction operates within the institutional domain of investments itself. The individual has, by and large, only one lifetime to think of, but society must consider both the short run and the long run. Thus, the alternatives for institutional investment in education range from the provision of short-term training courses, more or less with existing facilities, to the establishment of new schools and universities to serve, perhaps, several generations of students. I will return to the exact implication of the domain-distinction argument for the choice of the long-term and short-term categories of institutional investments in Chapter 4, with the presentation of examples based on the experiences of a number of countries. But let me first try to formulate the argument in terms of our own hypothetical example about the training prospects of these 100 science graduates for the technical degree.

Individual investment decisions of the science graduates would be guided, one might presume, by private calculations of private costs and benefits attributable to participation in the technical course along the lines suggested in Section 2.3. Institutional decisions, on the other hand, no matter how they are actually arrived at, would have to be socially judged on the basis of only social costs and benefits. The domain-distinction argument suggests in this context that this social judgment itself has to be in two parts.

First, the social costs and benefits of private investment decisions in the individual domain have to be estimated. These decisions will govern the individual actions of the students in securing their training through the technical course that may be provided, and the societal decision maker has to anticipate them. Second and, of course, more directly, one must estimate the social costs and benefits attributable to that institutional investment itself that will provide for the technical course. This implies, interestingly, that when one considers the usefulness of the information made available as "returns to education," one can think of *several* returns at the same time. In the case of the technical course, for example, one can think of (1) the private return as a possible guide to individual investment decisions (paying tuition, forgoing income-earning opportunities, etc.) for undertaking the course; (2) the social return from these individual investments, hopefully, as a possible guide to social policy with respect to the complementary institutional investments required; and, more directly, (3) the social return from these complementary investments themselves, that is, from constructing school buildings, recruiting teaching faculty, preparing material for the new course, etc., taking into account the social return expected from the concomitant individual investments.

Obviously, as far as the determination of the social return for the institutional investment component is concerned, the domain-distinction argument would tend to raise two questions at the same time: (a) To what extent does the estimate of the social return to investment in education in the institutional domain depend on the anticipation of concomitant investments in the individual domain, and (b) to what extent would the different time perspectives associated with different institutional investment opportunities in education permit the use of a single indicator of social return for all such investments? The first question refers to the "complementarity" and the second to the "diversity of time horizons" of investments discussed in the domain-distinction argument.

The former often implies a more basic but frequently encountered social-choice dilemma: whether to "provide for a group of individuals responding to a given set of institutional investments" or "provide for a different group expected to respond to a different set of institutional investments"?

The latter question also points to a basic social choice: "Provide a full-time technical course" or "provide in-service professional training," presumably for different sets of people.

I shall argue in Section 2.6 that the dilemmas exposed here through the consideration of the two distinct domains do not necessarily remain at the level of the domain-distinction argument but lead naturally to collective-choice questions. Similarly, in other instances the collective-choice argument could actually follow from dilemmas revealed by the micro–macro considerations that I discuss in the next section.[7]

## 2.5 The micro–macro argument: microparameters, microuncertainty, and macroeconomic calculations

Two broad considerations characterize the macroeconomic argument in the discussion of social policy with respect to investments in education. First, one must decide how far the parametric role of the rate of return to education usually attributed to it with respect to individual investment decisions can be expected to be retained for societal investments. The question becomes important both because in societal investments the scale of operation is often relatively large and, in general, because the aggregate of *all* investments in education – individual as well as societal investments – has to be considered for the total impact. We may call the former the *large investment* part and the latter the *aggregate investment* part of the question. As for the large-investment part, for example, suppose one has to ponder, when the relatively high present earnings of science graduates with the additional technical degree tempt government to start a new technical college, what the consequent *annual* addition to the number of trained professionals eventually would do to their future earnings. It is quite possible that the contemplated increment in investment for starting a new college would be so large for the size of the market that the rate of return itself, seen as one estimated magnitude, could collapse under its weight.

The more general aggregate-investment part of the question is, or *should* be, standard macroeconomics. That is, it is necessary to consider from society's point of view – and this also should be of some interest from the individual standpoint – not only what a single large chunk of societal investment can do, but also what the aggregate of *all* concomitant investments would do to the earnings of the technical degree holders. If too many science graduates decided to invest in the technical course, then the individual expectations, each possibly fully justified on the basis of their reading of the private rate-of-return tables, would together come to grief. So, of course, would societal expectations, if based on the same individual expectations of higher earnings. When faced with this prospect, it might be perfectly good macroeconomic sense on the part of the societal investor to disregard the favorable signaling of a relatively high marginal social rate of return, calculated in the conventional way, and to refuse to invest more in the form of a new technical college, for example, if the fear is that this will be accompanied by a totally unjustified increase in the aggregate of individual investments by masses of hopeful science graduates.

The second consideration in the argument is the distinction between the micro- and macrolevel uncertainties that have to be encountered in the course of investment decisions in education. Perhaps the most telling example of the implication of this distinction for social policy with respect to returns to education is as follows. Each science graduate in our example, it may be recalled, had a 90% probability of completing the technical course successfully, and thereafter again a 90% probability of getting the higher-paid job of a trained science graduate. This might, as I have suggested, induce each to lower his or her private estimate of the private rate of return corresponding to the technical degree by a fraction dependent on the probabilities of failure at the two levels. But obviously, this might leave the prospect bright enough for each of the science graduates wanting to invest in the technical-level training. And yet, the small probability of failure (.19) for each individual science graduate is clearly equivalent to the certainty of additional aggregate unemployment for the economy as a whole.

We thereby get into a hard-to-solve micro–macro dilemma for decision making in investment in education. If 100 science graduates intended to invest in the technical course on the basis of the estimate that 10 of them would fail to make it to the end of the course, and that of the 90 completing successfully, 9 would again lose out because only 81 of the higher-paid jobs were available, then surely each would be equally justified (or unjustified) in taking the plunge. Assuming that each had the same private uncertainties, he or she would have reduced the private rate of return in the same way. But the question before society is whether it would be equally justified at the macroeconomic level to use a *positive* marginal social rate of return having merely marked it downward on the basis of individual-level logic?[8]

If only 81 jobs at the technical degree level awaited the 90 successful trainees, then there can surely be a case for *not* allowing societal investment to create a capacity in the technical course for the intake of all 100 science graduates in the first place. This would be quite irrespective of what the marginal social rate of return, which is *positive*, though diminished by the probability of individual unemployment, might be thought to be signaling to the societal investor. And this would also be – and herein lies the dilemma – quite irrespective of the fact that each of the 100 individuals would be perfectly justified in wanting to invest in one of the 100 places in the technical course.

It may perhaps be argued that the fault here lies not with the marginal social rate of return but with the way it is calculated even when unemployment is a *certainty* in the aggregate. It may be suggested, for example, that if no better job opportunities were in prospect for all the people who could be trained, then the marginal social rate should really read as zero beyond an appropriate point of the contemplated outlay on that training. This is not shown on the conventional rate-of-returns tables only because the rates are linked to increments of schooling for a whole group rather than to increments of outlay. But if the marginal social rates of return *were* shown, perhaps more accurately in this manner, then it would be only another, more formal, way of showing that the omnibus rate-of-return approach did not work for societal decision making in the presence of aggregate unemployment, assuming that the availability of better-educated personnel did not reduce unemployment by itself.

The core of the micro–macro dilemma in this respect is that the social rate of return to schooling is an average. The marginal rate has to be shown as positive so long as there is improvement in the earnings of those who are schooled (at the particular level) all taken together, including those who would have no improvement in earnings at all. An additional societal investment in schooling would, therefore, appear socially profitable even when it was certain that it would add to the volume of educated unemployment at that level of schooling, provided the marginal social rates of return to alternative investments happened to be low enough.

Clearly then, the dilemma cannot be resolved merely by modifying the rate-of-return approach. In fact, the dilemma cannot be resolved at the level of the macroeconomic argument at all, which only helps to expose a more basic choice before the societal decision maker than that between alternative investment opportunities. To illustrate, the basic options for social choice can be seen in our example as follows: "Provide, at a given cost, education to eighty-one selected persons to prepare them for guaranteed employment in eighty-one higher jobs, leaving the remaining nineteen unemployed, or in less preferred jobs," or "Provide, at a higher cost, that education to all 100 persons, thereby ensuring for each person 81% probability of getting one of the higher jobs."

Whether it is this kind of social-choice dilemma or the dilemmas of the other kind that were revealed by the domain-distinction argument in the preceding section, what seems ultimately to be involved in all these problems is how to define the standpoint of society given the divergent individual points of view. This question is at the heart of the collective-choice argument to which I now turn.

## 2.6 The collective-choice argument: preferences and judgments

Though the collective-choice consideration should arise quite naturally in the treatment of the societal approach to investments in education, it is difficult to give the argument a completely specified structure. The argument applies to a large variety of choice situations and can, therefore, vary widely in content and form.[9] And yet, the collective-choice considerations have a welfare-economic character of their own that will distinguish them from the two other kinds of problems we have discussed.

First, there were the problems considered in Section 2.4, directly or indirectly involving the apportioning of investment decisions in education between the institutional and the individual domain. These can be seen as a class of equilibrium problems either directly related to the complementarity of the two domains, or indirectly related, caused by the divergent time perspectives in the institutional domain.

Second, equilibrium problems of another class arose when investment decisions based on individuals' microlevel assessments were contrasted with those based on macrolevel judgments. These problems were considered in Section 2.5 in the treatment of aggregate investment decisions in education.

Broadly speaking, except when it is explicitly introduced, one can say that the collective-choice argument arises implicitly whenever a consideration of the domain-distinction argument or the macroeconomic argument points to a paradoxical social-choice situation. Such paradoxes are encountered under many different conditions. I shall recall here three common instances.

First, take the case in which a positive signal is received from the market, based on microeconomic information, e.g., a relatively high marginal social rate of return to investment in the one-year technical course estimated as usual for the average graduate. But suppose that the signal clearly conflicts with a basic macroeconomic value judgment: "Investment that will create more unemployment is bad investment."

Second, suppose one gets two conflicting sets of signals that concern the same group of individuals. One set is conveyed through the operation of the market, with the message: "The marginal social rate of return to investment in the one-year technical course after graduation is relatively high compared to alternatives now available in the market." But the other message, conveyed through nonmarket channels (expert advice?) is as follows: "Improve the quality of education at the level of graduation itself; the marginal social rate of return will be higher here than in the lengthening of schooling by a year."

Finally, take the whole class of cases where interpersonal comparability problems arise because the set of signals emanating from the individual sources is itself heterogeneous. The paradox will be unavoidable if the set is an aggregation of diverse signals originating from different individuals or groups of individuals whose interests are affected in exactly opposite ways. Whichever way the aggregate signals are then read there is arbitrariness due to implicit or explicit interpersonal comparisons.

The purpose of the collective-choice argument is to expose the dilemmas in social choice that arise in these and, as we shall see in Chapter 4, similar situations because of the conflicts between the perception of self-interest at the individual level and the perception of either self-interest or social purpose of the same individuals at the collective level, or because of problems of interpersonal comparability between different individuals. Clearly, the argument is often more able to show *where* such conflicts are to be expected in a given situation and *why* analysis based on the assumption of homogeneity of investors in education would be suspect, than it is to say how an ensuing dilemma could be resolved. Since my object is merely to illustrate the collective-choice argument and not to exhaust it in the context of investments in education – an impossible task because of the multitude of specific forms it takes in specific situations – let me try to do so again in terms of our hypothetical example.

It may be recalled that our example concerned a group of 100 science graduates and the economics of their pursuing a one-year technical course after completion of their bachelor of science degree. Consider now the following scenario. The employers in the industry decide that a college graduate in science is more productive with an additional technical degree than without it. The technical degree holder, therefore, commands a higher salary than a mere science degree holder. On calculating the higher earning profile of the technical degree holder against the cost of the one-year course, including forfeited incomes, it is found that the marginal social rate of return to investment at the technical degree level is higher than that at the level of the plain bachelor of science degree. The societal investor is therefore tempted by the higher marginal social rate of return to devote additional resources to the introduction of the technical course, rather than to an expansion of the size of the science class.

Take a situation in which, let us say, it is also known to be the considered judgment of the employers that a *better-educated* science degree holder would have been just as good for their purpose as the *longer-educated* science graduate with a technical degree. But the employers find that there is no way they can reveal their relative preference through the choices they actually exercise in the labor market, though other ways are found to record it quite unambiguously in public. This leads to an inquiry, first into the nature of the improvement in the college graduate's education that the employers sought, and then into the cost of that improvement from the societal point of view. Suppose it is discovered that if given additional resources are spent on college education in science – not by supporting a larger number of students, but by allocating more inputs for the same number on some selected items of education (such as improved curriculum, better teaching), then the potential marginal social rate of return at the science degree level would be *higher* than that for the technical degree – *if* the employers are to be believed. The dilemma now is whether the employers or the observed factor-market prices are to be believed.

Two things seem to follow from this scenario. First, it is seen that societal investment decisions, if made on the basis of the marginal social rate of return derived in the usual manner as assumed in this example, would correspond to an aggregation of the employers' revealed preferences (over the set of alternative factor inputs) in the labor market. Second, it is also clear that such decisions can conflict with other societal preference orderings that could be equally legitimately arrived at through the aggregation of revealed judgments – in this case, of exactly the same individual employers. In this example, the individual judgments at issue happened to be the employers' judgments and these were not entirely subjective, being based on a factual assessment of the possibilities of improving the content of education for science graduates. In another case these could be simply value judgments.

Consider a second situation, for example, in which the individuals buying their education judge the quality of education imparted at the bachelor of science degree level to be appalling, making a value judgment uncontaminated by market considerations. They then all decide that more resources ought to be spent on it. But they also decide that institutional or societal investors rather than they themselves individually should spend the resources because the natural domain of the required investments was not individual but institutional. In other words, the individuals may want to behave as ordinary investors individually. But they may, at the same time behave collectively on a very different footing. In asking for better education at the science degree level they may be behaving partly as individual consumers of high-quality education without necessarily caring whether objectively it was all good personal investment. On the other hand, they may be behaving as societal investors who did not necessarily accept collectively the preferences they themselves revealed at the individual level. In either situation, the dilemma is whether the societal investor should be asked to go by the marginal social rate of return as reflected in the tables, favoring investment at the technical degree level, or by the individually or collectively expressed value judgments of employers or individuals who favor a higher quality of education at the science degree level?

The usual rate-of-return approach to investment in education, being basically linked to what might be called a strictly one-dimensional characterization of individuals' revealed preferences, gives no clue to handling the social-choice problem in either of the following two situations: (a) where some individuals are unable to reveal the "whole truth" through the market (as with the employers of the science graduates in our example), or (b) where the same individuals are inclined to reveal opposite preferences at the societal and the individual levels (as might happen with the science students themselves).[10]

I have suggested that the collective-choice argument, unless introduced explicitly, often arises only when the other arguments imply a breakdown of signals or a disequilibrium. This may not have been quite the most transparent observation to make, but it might still be interesting to check the assertion in concluding this chapter. Take, for example, the two situations described in the foregoing scenario. These can be seen from a fresh angle, that is, in terms of a failure at the level of the domain-distinction argument. To elaborate, the dilemma in the two situations can be described as arising because the market mechanism, because of its very nature, could permit only limited communication within or between the two domains: What the employers or the employees wished to convey could not be wholly conveyed through their choice behavior in the labor market.

In the second situation the dilemma can, moreover, be seen in terms of contradictory investment decisions made in the two domains – as a case of the *collection* of individual choices conflicting with the *collective* choice of the same individuals. In neither situation can the dilemma be resolved merely by recognizing the separation of individual and institutional domains. Hence arises the collective-choice argument involving the problems of aggregating individual preferences, reconciling the two different dimensions of individual interests and judgments, and, of course, selecting appropriate choice rules for arriving at societal decisions in investment in education.[11]

Similarly, if we go back to the macroeconomic argument and recall the dilemma raised by using the marginal social rate of return as the indicator of the social profitability of investment in education, which would be positive even when that very investment aggravated the unemployment problem for the educated, we can describe it now very differently. The marginal social rate of return to education, even when reduced by a coefficient in order to allow for the individual's probability of unemployment at that level of education, will still give a *positive* value. This can be shown to have one simple implication: If, behind a positive marginal social rate of return measured for a given level of education, there also existed a degree of unemployment at that level, then there must lie hidden at least *two* rates of return. One of the two must be even higher than the overall rate computed and would be earned by those who were happily employed – the eighty-one of the ninety trained science graduates in our example.

On the other hand, there must be at the same time a zero, or even a negative, rate earned by the unemployed. This implication would immediately raise two different interpersonal comparability questions. First, should society set the higher rate of return to the employed against the zero rate of return to the unemployed – both (perhaps random) results of the same aggregate institutional investment? Second, assuming that the total number of individuals in society is larger than the number of science graduates who are direct beneficiaries of the societal investment in education, should the rest of society be made to pay for the training of all 100 science graduates, knowing that only 81 of them would be employed at the level of their training?[12] It is again the task of the collective-choice argument to bring out and make explicit precisely questions like these. A macroeconomic disequilibrium will expose these issues, but the conventional rate-of-return approach to investments, devised for a *homogeneous* category of investors, would be in no position to accommodate, much less handle, them.

CHAPTER 3

# Rates-of-return tables in economics of education

## 3.1 Introduction

The basic tool of the rate-of-return approach to investment decisions in education is the rates-of-return table. This chapter is devoted to a detailed examination of this tool in the context of the arguments developed in Chapter 2.

The rates-of-return tables are drawn up for levels of formal education that are themselves determined by the number of years of schooling. Since economists of education have computed these tables essentially in only one way, it is useful for us to begin by understanding precisely what information the tables purport to convey.[1] My first concern in this chapter is how the rates are actually presented and what they signify. This is a different question from what economists expect these rates to represent in general, to which I shall turn next.[2]

I shall not raise here, however, any of the basic econometric questions such as those of the definition, the identification, and the measurability of the costs and benefits of education whether from the individual or the societal point of view, important as such questions are. These I presume have already been asked and dealt with at some other level. There can, of course, be obvious objection to taking on the rates-of-return table on this oversimplified basis, because it might well prove in the end to have led us on to an unrealistic exercise in economics. Even so, the purpose of that exercise should be clear enough: to clarify whether the rate of returns as presented in economics of education can indeed be regarded as an instrument (or index) of optimization in the same way as the rate of returns elsewhere would be. Claims to this effect, needless to say, have been made. Has it not been argued – sometimes quite openly and often at least implicitly – that economic efficiency requires the marginal rate of return to investment in education to be the same at each step of the educational ladder, *and* equal to the marginal rates of return to investment in physical capital everywhere else in the economy? Consider, for example, the following (Psacharopoulos, 1973; p. 7):

> Social efficiency, for example, requires equality between rates of return to investment in education at all levels and also that these are equal to the social rate of return on physical capital. Private efficiency has a similar meaning.

Then again, while interpreting an actual table:

> Regarding private efficiency, the near identity between private rates for secondary and higher education shows that from the individual points of view there has been, on average, the correct distribution of resources between these two levels.

Even if it is assumed that the initial questions of the definition, the identification, and the measurability of the return to education have all been resolved – within certain admitted limits of credibility and tolerance – it is necessary to make sure that we are really talking about, and comparing, the marginal rates of return to education within the same definitional framework used for the treatment of optimization of investment decisions elsewhere in the economy. Any question of the purported or desired equality or inequality of the different rates of return obviously becomes completely pointless otherwise.[3] This, then, is the major concern throughout the entire argument in this chapter. However, first, with regard to what I have just referred to as "the admitted limits of credibility and tolerance," that is, the acceptability of numbers shown on the rates-of-return tables as genuine surrogates for the returns to education, I will offer only a brief comment bearing on one basic aspect of the problem of definition, identification, and measurability in estimating the returns to education.

### *Productivity and earnings*

The arguments introduced in Chapter 2 would generally limit the scope of every possible kind of omnibus rate-of-return approach with regard to making individual investment decisions in education and would also lead one to seriously question the validity of making societal judgments on this basis. But for specific formulations there can be other considerations, less general but equally basic, that tend to limit the credibility that can be extended to some *particular* approach used in the representation of the rates of return. For example, the usual practice of computing the rates of return on the basis of the *incomes* of the individuals can be and has been singled out for such criticism.

Briefly, one's doubts about this particular way of representing the returns from education can arise in three stages. First, the possibility of widespread external economies suggests that the effects of an investment in education on the productivity of the educated are likely to make up only part of the total economic impact of that investment on the economy as a whole. Second, given a positive productivity effect of an investment in education, some of it may be held back by the employers and not reflected in increased earnings from the jobs of those who are directly being educated.[4] Conversely, all of the increased earnings seen to go with higher individual investments in education need not be due to education.[5] Third, changes in earnings are not the only changes represented in income data. Income arises from many sources, including earnings from jobs, and depends on individuals' assets as well as the jobs they hold.[6]

In spite of these well-known reservations, the contention that an individual's total income can be a dependable basis for calculating the returns from his or her education need not be wholly unjustified. There might be just enough *practical* justification since incomes, in contrast to earnings from a specified job, are not only very often the more easily observable, but also, by and large, the more convincing indicator of the individual's changed circumstances over time. But one must admit that this would be just enough justification, provided two things were clearly understood. First, one would have to bear in mind that since changes in the income profiles of the individuals did not necessarily reflect all the positive economic effects on society of an investment in education, one must be on the lookout for the other effects before deciding on social policy. Second, one must also consider the possibility that changes in incomes statistically associated with changes in the level of education do not necessarily indicate that an improvement in income was actually due to differential capability acquired by individuals through education alone. This could also be due to their other attributes (not even all necessarily commendable), such as their greater command over initial capital endowment or their superior social position or connections, any or all of which could possibly both encourage them to make a higher outlay on education, and extract a higher return for it.

With no more than these cursory references to the possible limits of credibility and tolerance to the conceptual acceptance of the figures as rates of return to investment in education, I now turn to the actual tables that economists of education compute and on which their analysis of investments in education usually rests.

## 3.2 Hansen's tables

The rates-of-return tables are based on the available (cross-sectional) data on lifetime income profiles of groups of individuals on the benefits side. On the cost side, figures are computed for the direct and attributed components of the costs of education presumed to be actually incurred, and the opportunity costs of income forgone as a result of the time spent on education.

Before proceeding further with this commentary, I must now bring in as exhibits actual tables constructed on the basis of educational costs data and age–income profiles of given groups of educated individuals. For these I will turn to Hansen (1963), who first provided the tables for the rates of return to investment in schooling in the United States for 1949.[7] I take up Hansen's calculations in some detail below because, apart from being an early contribution to the methodology of constructing the tables, these are also fair samples of the many similar calculations in this field that have appeared over the past two decades, some of the most important of which are discussed or referred to, for example, in Woodhall (1970) and Psacharopoulos (1973). Some important reservations about the basis of calculations of the Hansen-type tables, it must be pointed out, have been expressed, and a number of consequent adjustments in many of the later calculations of the rates of return have since been both suggested and made.[8] For example, the private and social rates of return to education for the urban male population of India were calculated by Blaug, Layard, and Woodhall (1969) after making adjustments for innate individual differential ability (the so-called $\alpha$-factor, for which they used alternative arbitrary values), the probability of a given stretch of unemployment after graduation, and a 2% growth rate per year in Indian incomes. Although some of these adjustments themselves might make matters worse – I have tried to show how the adjustment for the probability of unemployment runs afoul of the micro–macro argument – these do not affect the basic conceptual structure of the information shown in the tables.

The three tables reproduced in this chapter are all based on estimates of resource costs of education for different levels of schooling and the cross-sectional data on age–income patterns at the corresponding levels of education. The cost streams are established over the period of schooling at each level, and consequent improvement in lifetime income prospects are estimated for each successive level. The lifetime cost–income stream attributed to a given level of schooling is then taken as the difference between the cost–income profile of the average individual for that level and the income profile for the immediately preceding level.

As an example, we will take four years of college beginning at age eighteen. The cost-income profile would show, to the end of age twenty-one, perhaps only costs – both school costs and school-related costs – but no income. Thereafter, there would be only the (supposedly) higher income profile of the successful college graduate. This must now be reduced by the lifetime opportunity cost incurred through not joining the work force at the age of eighteen, which is measured by the observed income profile of high school graduates from age eighteen onward. Thus, the difference between the two profiles becomes the lifetime cost–income stream attributed to four years of college education. The corresponding rate of return is then estimated by finding the rate of discount that equates the present value of the cost stream and the present value of the income stream that is, the two components of the lifetime cost-income stream attributed to four years of college education.

Hansen himself clearly expressed many of the reservations that must qualify any acceptance of his rate-of-return estimates at their face value as reliable measures of the contribution of schooling to personal earnings. First was the well-known question of an unidentified component of unearned income remaining entangled with earnings in the income profile. Since there was likely to be a positive association between greater wealth and higher levels of schooling in the first place, the rate of return measured by income would overestimate the contribution of schooling alone. Second, different socioeconomic groups were often found to be concentrated at the two extremes of the spectrum of educational levels, such as blacks and Puerto Ricans with little schooling at one end and more favored social groups at the other. This obviously undermined the usefulness of the cross-sectional data for estimating changes in the earnings levels of persons corresponding to changes in their educational levels. Third, the contribution of higher intrinsic merit of the individuals that often went with higher investments in education (in the present sense of going further up the educational ladder) was not separated from the contribution of education in the income profiles. Fourth, no allowance could be made in the calculations for the direct consumption aspect of education. If this proved to be different for the different levels of education, then clearly the relative rates of return to investment would not be correctly shown by data on costs and relative earnings. Fifth, there was the statistical problem: The cross-sectional data had to be assumed to be holding steady over lifetimes in a way that would leave at least the relative rates of return unaffected. Sixth, there were other factors possibly affecting relative rates of return that did not enter into the calculation of the rates-of-return tables at all.

Obviously, the objections anticipated by Hansen indeed make a formidable list. In fact, in addition to the aforementioned objections, Hansen mentioned two other factors: the probability of unemployment and the probability of mortality as affecting the reliability of the calculations. Although anticipating the objections does not necessarily mean that they are also taken care of, it might be cited in justification of the course that I shall now follow. I shall assume that the rate-of-return calculations were all duly corrected, somehow, for all the preceding factors and then try to read them.

Hansen uses two major variants in the calculation of the resource costs of education: (a) the total resource costs from the societal point of view, and (b) the private resource costs from the standpoint of individuals paying for their own or some other individual's education. The total resource cost – or what may more familiarly be called the social cost – comprises three components: (1) direct (net) school costs for such items as teachers' salaries, teaching material, buildings, etc., incurred by (i.e., on behalf of) society; (2) school-related costs incurred by the individuals for travel, books, and equipment, etc.; and (3) costs incurred by individuals as a result of the schooling involved, in the shape of incomes forgone from the point of entering school.

As for the private resource costs, these also obviously have components 2 and 3, though for the first component, the direct school costs incurred by *society* are to be replaced by the direct (net) school costs incurred by *individuals* in the form of tuition and other fees.

It will be noted that these tables do not distinguish between societal and individual considerations for calculating the benefits or the gross returns; they do so only when calculating the costs. The additions to the lifetime income streams of individuals receiving the schooling are the only measure of the gross return, whether for the individuals themselves or for society. Subject to this, internal rates of return to total resource investment (Table 3.1) would refer to social rates of return, and internal rates of return to private resources investment (*before* tax in Table 3.2; *after* tax, adjusting only for the federal income tax, in Table 3.3) would refer to private returns to education over the relevant years of schooling.

## 3.3 Marginal returns to investment

The major difficulty in interpreting the information shown on these tables, even when one accepts it as a fair representation of average returns to investment, lies in deciding exactly where, and how, to represent the marginal investment decisions. The difficulty persists whether one looks at it from the standpoint of private individuals buying their education, or from the point of view of society for evaluating institutional investments providing schooling for the individuals. There is, in fact, more than a mere semantic difficulty involved here with the use of the term "marginal." This has to be cleared up first if one is to avoid becoming confused later when talking about comparing the different alternative margins of investment decisions, including the investment decisions in education.

The confusion in usage, discussed in some detail in Section 3.4, is briefly as follows. The margin of investment, in normal economic usage, lies where investors consider *small* increments in their total outlay on a particular line of investment. In the rate-of-return literature in economics of education, however, the *marginal increment in outlay* refers to the amount necessary at a given level of education to provide or buy an additional *quantum of schooling* (measured in length of time). This is meant to take the individual to the next higher level of education. This distinction of usage creates a problem of interpretation even when analysis is confined to comparing

Table 3.1. *Internal rates of return to total resource investment in schooling in the United States for males (1949)*

| | From: | | (1) | (2) | (3) | (4) | (5) | (6) | (7) |
|---|---|---|---|---|---|---|---|---|---|
| | | | 6 | 8 | 12 | 14 | 16 | 18 | 20 |
| To: | Age | Grade | 1 | 3 | 7 | 9 | 11 | 13 | 15 |
| (1) | 7 | 2 | 8.9 | — | — | — | — | — | — |
| (2) | 11 | 6 | 12.0 | 14.5 | — | — | — | — | — |
| (3) | 13 | 8 | 15.0 | 18.5 | 29.2 | — | — | — | — |
| (4) | 15 | 10 | 13.7 | 15.9 | 16.3 | 9.5 | — | — | — |
| (5) | 17 | 12 | 13.6 | 15.4 | 15.3 | 11.4 | 13.7 | — | — |
| (6) | 19 | 14 | 11.3 | 12.1 | 11.1 | 8.2 | 8.2 | 5.4 | — |
| (7) | 21 | 16 | 12.1 | 12.7 | 12.1 | 10.5 | 10.9 | 10.2 | 15.6 |

*Note*: All rate-of-return figures are subject to some error, since the estimation to one decimal place was made by interpolation between whole percentage figures.
*Source*: Hansen (1963).

investments made within the education sector on different lines or levels of education. Moreover, when the purpose of analysis is to carry over comparisons between marginal investment decisions in the education sector to comparisons with marginal investment decisions everywhere else in the economy, the definitional difficulty becomes absolutely critical, because then it is no longer permissible to cling to separate terminology reserved for the representation of costs and returns in education alone.

Let us now examine the tables. In each, the first figure in the last seven columns is the rate corresponding to each successive increment of schooling by specified periods. These are interpreted as the *marginal rates of return*. For example, the marginal social rate of return to the first two years of elementary school (for U.S. males in 1949) is 8.9% and to the last two years of college, 15.6% (Table 3.1). The marginal private rate of return to the first two years of elementary school is infinite, being assumed costless to the private individual, and 16.7% to the last two years of college, after allowing for federal income taxes (Table 3.3). The "average" rates over periods comprising more than one time interval or educational level are also shown. For example, the average social rate of return to six years of elementary schooling as shown in Table 3.1, is the average, weighted by the respective outlays, of the marginal rate for the first two years (8.9%) and the marginal rate for the next four years (14.5%), and calculated at 12.0%.

Table 3.2. *Internal rates of return to private resource investment in schooling before tax in the United States for males (1949)*

| | From: | | (1) | (2) | (3) | (4) | (5) | (6) | (7) |
|---|---|---|---|---|---|---|---|---|---|
| | | | 6 | 8 | 12 | 14 | 16 | 18 | 20 |
| To: | Age | Grade | 1 | 3 | 7 | 9 | 11 | 13 | 15 |
| (1) | 7 | 2 | † | — | — | — | — | — | — |
| (2) | 11 | 6 | † | † | — | — | — | — | — |
| (3) | 13 | 8 | † | † | † | — | — | — | — |
| (4) | 15 | 10 | 28.3 | 34.6 | 25.9 | 12.7 | — | — | — |
| (5) | 17 | 12 | 25.6 | 29.4 | 23.3 | 15.3 | 18.6 | — | — |
| (6) | 19 | 14 | 18.1 | 18.7 | 14.8 | 10.4 | 9.5 | 6.2 | — |
| (7) | 21 | 16 | 18.2 | 18.7 | 16.2 | 12.9 | 13.0 | 11.6 | 18.7 |

*Note*: All rate-of-return figures are subject to some error, since the estimation to one decimal place had to be made by interpolation between whole percentage figures. † indicates an infinite rate of return, given the assumption that education is costless to the individual to the completion of eighth grade.
*Source*: Hansen (1963).

Hansen, and others who have worked with similar tables (e.g., Blaug 1970, Woodhall 1970, Psacharopoulos 1973, and the numerous studies referred to by them), usually read these marginal rates of return to education exactly as if reading the marginal rates of return for the capital market. In fact, the whole point of their exercise would have been lost if they had not, because the purpose was to establish the comparability of the marginal rates of return at the various levels both between themselves, and with the marginal rates of return to other kinds of investment. It is necessary, therefore, to examine carefully what exactly is involved in the claims to such comparability. Hansen himself interpreted the figures in Table 3.1 in an absolutely straightforward – and rather simplistic – way:

Evidence such as this on the marginal or incremental rates of return is ordinarily used in discussing resource allocation. . . . At an alternative return to society, of say, 10 per cent, investment in all grade levels except the last three would be justified. Were the alternative rate, say, 7 per cent, only the last level would be excluded.[9]

Similarly, he interpreted the figures in Tables 3.2 and 3.3 in the following manner:

When individuals and/or their parents plan an investment programme in schooling, the private rates of return justify securing more schooling than do the rates of return on total resources investment. For example, the

Table 3.3. *Internal rates of return to private resource investment in schooling after tax in the United States for males (1949)*

| | From: | | (1) | (2) | (3) | (4) | (5) | (6) | (7) |
|---|---|---|---|---|---|---|---|---|---|
| | | | 6 | 8 | 12 | 14 | 16 | 18 | 20 |
| To: | Age | Grade | 1 | 3 | 7 | 9 | 11 | 13 | 15 |
| (1) | 7 | 2 | † | — | — | — | — | — | — |
| (2) | 11 | 6 | † | † | — | — | — | — | — |
| (3) | 13 | 8 | † | † | † | — | — | — | — |
| (4) | 15 | 10 | 27.9 | 33.0 | 24.8 | 12.3 | — | — | — |
| (5) | 17 | 12 | 25.2 | 28.2 | 22.2 | 14.5 | 17.5 | — | — |
| (6) | 19 | 14 | 17.2 | 17.5 | 13.7 | 9.4 | 8.5 | 5.1 | — |
| (7) | 21 | 16 | 17.2 | 17.3 | 14.4 | 11.5 | 11.4 | 10.1 | 16.7 |

*Note*: All rate-of-return figures are subject to some error, since the estimation to one decimal place had to be made by interpolation between whole percentage figures. † indicates an infinite rate of return, given the assumption of costless education to the individual through the completion of eighth grade.
*Source*: Hansen (1963).

marginal rates of return to elementary, high-school, and college schooling are infinite (Table 3.2: col. 1, row 3), 15.3 per cent (col. 4, row 5), and 11.6 per cent (col. 6, row 7), respectively. Thus investment in schooling through college is still profitable even if the private alternative rate is as high as 11.5 per cent. But on an after-tax basis, the alternative rate of 10 per cent just permits private investment at the college level (Table 3.3: col. 6, row 7).[10]

I should point out, however, that not all users of the rates-of-return tables have been equally determined in pushing the optimization exercise for educational investments to the hilt, though they all must have considered the marginal rates as fairly useful indicators for arriving at reasonably correct societal judgment on investment decisions. Blaug (1970), however, notes *two* distinct difficulties in the marginal private rates of return, though he absolves the marginal social rates. First, on the terminological aspects of the marginal and the average as applied to the rates of return to schooling he observes:

The meaning of the terms 'average' and 'marginal' in this context are sometimes confused. The marginal rates in Hansen's tables are marginal in the sense that they refer to an increment of schooling but since they are computed from age cohort data they are averages for particular age groups: they do not show what would happen if an additional student were provided with an extra year of education; they are not rates of return on increments of schooling for the marginal student. This is a serious limitation from the point of view of the individual since he can never be sure whether he is himself representative of his own age cohort. It is no drawback, however, for social policy which in any case cannot be framed for each and every individual case.[11]

Blaug also touches upon a second difficulty in comparing the marginal private rates of return stemming from the consideration that individuals' assessments of their investment opportunities in education at the successive levels are not mutually independent:

It has been suggested that we ought really to add at each stage of the educational ladder the cash value of the option to obtain still more education, suitably weighted by the probability of the option being exercised. . . . But despite the fact that different levels of education are successive investments for the individual, they are not independent investment projects from the standpoint of social policy; provided sufficient numbers of students are actually enrolled in the various levels, each level can be marginally expanded or contracted independently of every other. Thus, marginal rates of return are usually more pertinent in evaluating public expenditure on education by levels or years of schooling.[12]

Blaug's comments deserve careful attention because they would apply to the rates-of-return analysis in education in general, including the more recent and more refined versions available in Blaug (1970), Woodhall (1970), and Psacharopoulos (1973), and because they are also valid. However, I shall try to show, with some help from the arguments introduced in Chapter 2, that they also roundly miss the point about the real difficulty with the comparability of the marginal rates of return that seems to be involved in each instance. Let me now take them up one by one in the following two sections.

## 3.4 Increment of schooling and increment of outlay

First, take the point about the marginal rate of return calculated for an increment of schooling. Blaug rightly points out that the tables give the return for the *average* student of an age cohort rather than for the marginal student, and this return is, therefore, in that sense, an average rate of return for any given increment of schooling. Consequently, it is also true that particular individuals or marginal students would not know how to read the marginal rate as given on the table for their own purposes, unless they have already taken a view of – or have an additional clue to – their relative position in the league.[13] This is an important point to make, but can we say that uncertainty of this kind is a peculiar feature of individual investment decisions in education and is rare in other kinds of investment decisions? The truth, on the contrary, is that in all kinds of individual investments made under conditions of uncertainty, decision makers have to make guesses at least at *two* different levels. First, they must take a view of the market by trying to read the future from the tables based on the past. Second, they must decide on the size of their own stake in the game – their scale – for which they need to estimate how high (or how low) they will be when the returns are finally brought in, either as better-than-average or worse-than-average performers in the market. On both counts, individual investment decisions in education should be, if anything, rather *less* subject to the kind of wide (even wild) dispersal of the probable value of returns – from fairly high to negative – that confronts investment decisions in other markets of the economy.

Blaug is also probably wrong in thinking that, in the circumstances described, the marginal rates should make more sense for social policy than for individual decisions. It is true that, as he points out, society does not have to worry about the vicissitudes of any particular individual's career: The social purpose is effectively served if the table of returns is approximately correct on the whole, that is, for the average or the representative individual. But the societal decision maker can still be very wrong and the individual quite reasonably justified in viewing the rate of return as a dependable indicator for the simple reason that the two sets of investments involved are not of the same kind.

To recall the domain-distinction argument presented in Section 2.4, societal investment decisions in education (such as setting up new schools, training new teachers) stand in contrast to *individual* investment decisions (accepting admission to a school, registering for yet another year, and so on). The former, by their very nature, are likely to be relatively large. They sometimes may be too large, as the macroeconomic argument in Section 2.5 suggested, for the rate of return to behave as a useful parameter except perhaps in the very short run. But societal investment decisions in education are seldom in fact so conveniently short term, whereas individual decisions often are.

Thus, the upper bounds of the two sets of time horizons involved in the two domains are invariably widely different. The individual invests in education for up to one lifetime. Society invests in the education of individuals, sometimes for several generations at once. Clearly, therefore, if there were any uncertainty about which way the marginal rate of return would go in the future, individuals might be in a much better position to use the current information for their kind of small investment decisions than society would for its large investment decisions.

To return to Blaug's comment, the distinction he does *not* bring out is that the marginal rates in the tables are marginal in the special sense that they refer to increments of schooling and not to increments of outlay. This is where the difficulty lies, and not really in having to decide whether to call the rate of return marginal or average; nor is it in finding out whether the private individual or the maker of social policy could make the more satisfactory use of the tables. It is because of this very difficulty that a rate-of-return table cannot, for example, answer correctly the following simple question: What returns can I expect if I put in an additional £100 at a given level of schooling? It cannot, unless that £100 happens to be exactly the amount necessary to buy me a *quantum* increment in schooling. This is not how I should expect to read the marginal rates of return in other alternative ways of investing my resources, and it is *one* problem of comparability. Let me turn to another.

Since the tables show rates of return in terms of discrete jumps of levels of schooling, they implicitly assume for the individual, investments that are not only not finely divisible but also more or less fixed for any given level. It also happens that the amounts needed for the different levels of schooling are usually of all different sizes. To recall an illustration introduced in Section 2.2, suppose that I can buy for my family an increment of schooling at level *A* (primary education) for Rs. 100 per year and an increment of schooling at level *B* (higher education) for Rs. 1,000 per year. Suppose also that the table shows that both levels give the same (say, 10%) marginal private rate of return. The table does *not* show that to earn the same rates I have to invest in *B ten* times (and *only* ten times) the resources that I need to invest in *A*. Surely this is not quite the message I get if I am told, when I consider other ways of investing my resources, that the same 10% return is expected from two alternative channels. Hence arises that other problem of comparability: Each marginal rate of return implicitly assumes a (possibly) different size of the increment in individual investment.

On both counts it should be clear that economists do not usually describe the rate of returns to investment in the way the rate of returns to investment in education has been described here. In fact, the term bears so little resemblance to the ones economists are used to (e.g., the "rate of return" proposed by Solow [1963]) that perhaps a different nomenclature would have been less confusing.[14]

To sum up, the problem of comparability of the marginal rates of return in different alternative channels of investment cannot possibly be overcome unless *one* of two conditions is fulfilled: (a) Increments in the outlay of resources are reasonably finely divisible, (b) if they are not, they will be of reasonably similar size in the alternative channels of investment.

The first condition is often met when one considers the alternative investment possibilities in the capital market. The second condition is similarly often found to hold when we are able to appraise investment possibilities of a given outlay in alternative "projects." But unfortunately, the tables satisfy neither of the alternative conditions of comparability for the individual investor.

## 3.5 Interdependence of investments in schooling

Let me now turn to the second comment I quoted from Blaug (1970), which refers to an implied dependence of the marginal rate of return at each level of schooling, on the marginal rates of return expected at *subsequent* levels. Presumably, one reason I might want to get started at a certain level of education would be that I wanted the benefits I hoped to derive from the education at the next higher subsequent level.

One way of taking this dependence into account would be, as Blaug correctly observes, to follow the suggestion of Weisbrod (1964), for example, of calculating what I may call a *truer* marginal rate of return to schooling at a given level. One can do this by adding to the rate shown on the tables the cash value of the advantage calculated on the basis of the probability of entry into the subsequent level of schooling and its estimated effect on the individual's cost–income stream.[15] Blaug points out that another way would be to rely on the average rate of return to schooling over the two levels, which would be the weighted average of the corresponding marginal rates as shown on the tables. Though Blaug mentions that this would be the standard method (see Ribich, 1968,

Appendix C) of lumping together interdependent investments, he fails to note that resorting to the standard method cuts the Gordian knot of the comparability question by eliminating the idea of comparisons between levels of schooling in the first place.

Blaug, however, asserts that neither method of dealing with interdependent investments is really necessary when the question is viewed in terms of social policy. Provided sufficiently large numbers had been enrolled at all the levels, society should always find it possible and useful to consider marginal expansions or contractions of these numbers at any one level independent of any other. This observation, of course, is both valid and important for short-term policy, but a question remains to be asked for the longer run – a question that comes up in our macroeconomic argument. Would society be justified in assuming that the marginal rates of return to schooling at the various levels would themselves be independent of one another even if one granted that marginal expansions or contractions of the numbers could *start* at one level independent of another?

Let me provide an illustration. It is known, let us say, that the marginal social rate of return to investment in primary education in India is higher than to investment in higher education. Suppose also that it is known that the major component of the cost of investment in Indian primary education is teachers' salaries. And finally, suppose that salary rates of Indian primary school teachers, themselves products of the higher-education sector, are determined by the opportunity earnings of college graduates, which in turn are also a determinant of the marginal rate of return to investment in higher education. Now, if we reduce investment in higher education in India by reducing the number of seats in colleges, presumably because the marginal rate of returns in higher education was considered too low, then there might be fewer teachers available for the primary schools.

Whether this possibility is described in terms of a shortage of teachers (at current salaries) or a rise in the cost of primary education and, therefore, a fall in the marginal rate of return to primary education, the net result is likely to be a fall in primary schooling and possibly a consequent fall in the numbers at that level – a result scarcely to be expected if the two levels were independent. This is the crux of the difficulty with the interdependence of the levels of schooling with regard to long-term social policy. And this difficulty is not solved by the initial ability, in the short run, of societal investors to expand or contract numbers at different levels independent of one another.

Once again, Blaug's line of reasoning seems to miss the main point about the interdependence of investments in education; that is, it affects decision making for individuals and for society in their respective domains in completely different ways. Let me briefly recapitulate this distinction.

So far as the individual investor is concerned, it will be remembered that the interdependence of investment follows from the hierarchical character of the formal system of education itself. The system ensures that investments in schooling at successive levels can only be made in a strict sequence so that individuals do not see them as alternative opportunities at any given point of decision making. This implies a lexicographical ordering of investment opportunities over time, and this is the main factor from an individual point of view standing in the way of comparability of the marginal rates of return to investment in schooling at two different levels. Compared to this basic difficulty, Blaug's point about the underestimation of the marginal rate at a given level because of failure to assess the possibility of entry into the higher levels would not be such an irremediable defect. Provided the probabilities of entry into the higher levels can be estimated reasonably well, all that would be required is to revise the rates upward appropriately. In fact, if the probability of entry into the higher level did not vary greatly between levels for a given individual, then the exercise may even leave the relative rates unchanged.

From the standpoint of social policy, the interdependence between investments in the different levels of schooling resulting from their *sequential* nature might not be of great concern since, as has been seen, it may be possible to consider expanding or contracting the numbers at any one level independently of any other. The interdependence that mattered societally, however, was the input–output–input kind of relationship that seemed to exist between the sectors and that made the viability of the investment in the primary sector of education, for example, dependent on the availability of graduates from the higher-education sector. This was the macro part of the micro–macro argument involved in our hypothetical (but not improbable) illustration drawn from the Indian experience. I must add that this argument would also invariably lead to a collective-choice argument to remind the societal decision maker that the welfare of a group directly benefiting from institutional or societal investment in education at one level (primary, for example, as in the illustration) was not necessarily comparable to the welfare of a different group that would stand to benefit from an investment in the institutional domain at another level (say, higher education). This consideration would also be complicated by the complementarity implied in the input–output–input kind of interdependence between the two levels.

## 3.6 Returns to nonformal education

A discussion on the usefulness of the rate-of-return approach in educational investment would be incomplete without reference to nonformal education or, more accurately, the general case under which the structure of education is itself not assumed to be necessarily one of formal schooling.

The private rate of return, in the case of nonhuman capital, is a good accounting index of what past investment decisions yielded for the individual investor. Its use, however, not only as an efficiency index of *past* investment decisions, but also as a signal for *impending* investment decisions, requires a few additional assumptions. For example, as is well known, the translation from the observed to the expected rate of return to investment – or the marginal efficiency of investment – needs to take into account the state of expectation in the market. Similarly, if the purpose is to look at investment decisions societally, there are problems in translating the private into the social rate of return.

Clearly then, there are at least two levels of difficulties to overcome if the task is to obtain a rate of return to investment in education that would provide both an efficiency index for the past and a usable signal for future societal investment decisions. At each of these two levels the analogy between the returns to physical capital and the returns to human capital is more severely strained if the assumption of a formal system of education is dropped.

First, consider the expectations regarding the rate of returns. On the costs side, one could perhaps make the same useful approximations and imputations that are made for counting the expected costs of any other kind of social investment. Estimating the costs for education, therefore, should not pose greater problems in this respect. But, on the benefits side, one usually has to make the broad assumption that the net returns to education are all duly reflected in the increased individual earnings of the immediate beneficiaries.

Now, in the formal education system, the task of estimating the net returns from the expected increases in earnings is at least formally manageable. For example, let us say that a given number of years in medical school, involving a certain stream of expenditure and of income forgone, will produce a medical doctor. This representative doctor can be given a lifetime earnings profile estimated from either past profiles of medical doctors or cross-sectional studies of their earnings. The individual or the societal investor can thereby have a basis for making their own estimates of the expected rate of return, though they would probably vary their estimates with the state of expectation in the market, the degree of confidence, and other such factors. But how does one pursue the streams of expected returns from investment in a multipurpose education program in terms of lifetime earnings of the various categories of people directly involved, whose benefits may not even be separable in the first place? Second, whose lifetime earnings should one really try to count, realizing that the whole point about a particular nonformal program might be the large size of its *externalities*? This points to the *other* difficulty, that is, deriving the social from the private rate or return. The difficulty is naturally aggravated when externalities are expected to dominate.

The rate-of-return approach, then, must fulfill at least two practical requirements before the usefulness of the analogy in the field of education can be admitted. First, an activity must be identified within a process of education that is seen to be a distinct investment activity, not overlapping with other investment activities and leading to its own *uniquely* spelled out sequence of returns in terms of the increased earnings of a well-defined set of beneficiaries. Second, the external benefits of the investment activity that do not appear in the form of increased earnings of some or other identifiable sets of beneficiaries must not be large. In the case of the medical doctor or a graduate engineer in a formal system of education, these requirements are perhaps fulfilled, at least from the viewpoint of the individual investor.

Thus, a medical education might be seen to be more (or less) profitable than an engineering education in terms of the respective rates of returns. The discrimination between the two might be possible since each is seen as a more or less unique articulation over time in terms of sequences of decisions and outcomes and the two fields do not overlap. Also, the benefits measured in terms of the earnings of the doctors or the engineers may perhaps be assumed to capture the larger part of the benefits due to their education. A process of nonformal education, on the other hand, would be too flexible – having no unique articulation of a sequence of decisions and outcomes – and should have at least some objectives that would be as important as improvements in the earnings of the direct beneficiaries. In addition, a program of nonformal education would often aim at more than one target group, so that the average rate of return calculated could not be useful to any *one* group of investors as a guide to their investment decisions.

## 3.7 Summing up: Whose returns are they talking about?

The limits of the rate-of-return approach are fairly firmly set by a consideration common to each of the three broad categories of arguments highlighted in this study. It would have been noted that for each of the categories, there is one crucial question: Who was the decision maker or, alternatively, who was the prospective beneficiary? The implication of this question basically limits the rate-of-return approach. In the domain-distinction argument, for example, one had to determine whether the investment contemplated was in the decision-making domain of the individual or in the institutional or societal domain. For the micro–macro argument the question was whether the logic of decision making was to be the relevant logic for individuals or was it to be the logic for the economy as a whole. Again, the collective-choice argument raised a similar question for examining the social-choice problems that originated in the differences in preferences and judgments of the different decision makers in the economy.

The crux of the matter, in other words, is that whichever of the three types of arguments is taken into account, the set of decision makers cannot conceivably be taken as a homogeneous whole. For this reason, any omnibus rate-of-return approach is bound to be inadequate whatever its refinements. An omnibus rate of return is bound to prove a blunt instrument in the sense that it cannot discriminate between the different purposes of the different (individual and institutional or societal) decision makers.

Coming now from the general to the particular, we have noted in this chapter a number of specific limitations of the Hansen-type tables based on years-of-schooling limitations pointed out by many economists, beginning with Hansen himself. All these and similar objections perhaps can best be summarized under the following three heads.

### *The rates do not imply alternative opportunities*

From the standpoint of individual decisions, the tables only give information on rates of return to investment for levels of education that must be taken by the individual *in a strict sequence*. Therefore, this was not operationally relevant at any given point in decision making.

From the social point of view the input–output–input relationships between sectors of education complicate straight comparisons of rates of return.

### *The rates are not marginal*

The marginal rate of returns to investment in education as shown in the conventional tables is not marginal as understood in normal economics usage. First, the marginal investment does not refer to a small increment in outlay but rather to a quantum increment in outlay required for the relevant increment in the length of schooling. Second, the quantum of marginal investment is widely different for the different levels of schooling. Third, from the standpoint of the individual investor the marginal investment has to be one shot and is not ordinarily repeatable.

### *The rates are not optimal*

A given rate of return shown on the table is not necessarily the best rate for that particular level available to the average investor. For example, possible returns from investment in the quality of education at a given level (rather than proceeding to the next higher level) are not considered.[16]

### *A concluding remark*

Finally, let me conclude this chapter by adding a word on one implication that did *not* follow from the foregoing analysis. I have suggested that the marginal rates of return to investment in education were not in the same category as marginal rates of return to investment as understood in normal economics usage, at least since Solow (1963). The conclusion, therefore, is that this would not be a dependable instrument for an optimal investment policy that could be adopted by *any* decision maker, whether individual or institutional – contrary to what has often been claimed. But this is not tantamount to making, at the same time, the counterclaim that the kind of information on costs and benefits that had to be or could be collected for the construction of the tables would not be useful. As the criticisms of the omnibus rate of return would immediately suggest, a more comprehensive and segmented set of indicators of return would be required if all three levels of arguments introduced in Chapter 2 had to be taken into account for societal investment decisions in education. For that task, too, the primary information generated and collected by the conventional rate-of-return approach, though not, perhaps, the final tables themselves, would surely have to be regarded as crucial.

CHAPTER 4

# Social-choice problems in education

## 4.1 Introduction

If a straightforward rate-of-returns approach is ruled out, then what other kind of analysis can societal judgments on investment in education be based on? The purpose of this chapter is to examine six "real-life" examples and an alternative framework of analysis suggested by the three basic arguments of this study, that is, domain distinction, the distinction of microeconomic and macroeconomic logic, and the considerations of collective choice. The examples are actually stylized versions of a number of studies reported in the literature and are based on the experiences of a number of countries. No attempt has been made here deliberately to seek out an example where *a* social choice problem was particularly or explicitly identified by the formulators of the program or the author of the study concerned. This, of course, has left each of the examples a little more rough-hewn than one would have wished, even after considerable chipping away at the original mass of information. But that, after all, cannot be a sign of their weakness.

The difficulties, on the other hand, that one must contend with in interpreting the examples so as to identify the social-choice problems involved in them are quite substantial even in these simplified versions. Two difficulties are obvious, and a methodological point needs to be made about them at the very outset: Specifically, making the nature of the social-choice problem in educational investment explicit separately and in detail in different types of situations, rather than providing a homogeneous criterion (or even a set of criteria) admissible for all situations, must be seen as the main purpose of economic analysis.

In the first place, one has to contend with the fact that social-choice problems do not easily fall into a set pattern; or in any case, they do not fall into a pattern that is instantly or necessarily recognized by the concerned individual or institutional investor in a fully articulate manner. Moreover, in education, as in other kinds of social investment, the problem is to arrive at a social judgment quite irrespective of the investment motivations of the particular decision maker. But for arriving at a social judgment on investments, as contrasted with private judgments made in one's immediately discernible self-interest, the nature of the "maximand" itself, if any, might not be clearly foreseen by the decision maker concerned. This makes identifying the different and contending strands in the social-choice question to that extent more difficult.

The second difficulty is that what constitutes a social-choice problem also remains, by itself, a matter of basic value judgment for the onlooker. This implies that though one might visualize a set of possible social-choice problems involved in an instance, one could proceed further only by arbitrarily accepting a value judgment that a given situation of discovered conflict – whether of interests or of judgments – constitutes the relevant social-choice problem.

However, the two difficulties imply only the great variety of social-choice problems to be anticipated and not necessarily any great arbitrariness in their statement. Specifically, the three basic arguments can be stated as arguments of positive economics to an extent. To that extent, at least the *basis* for anticipating a set of social-choice problems in a situation could also be set down without arbitrariness. On the strength of this methodological point I now turn to the examples.

Example 1 (Section 4.2) is based on the Brazilian Intensive Program for the Preparation of Industrial Labor. Example 2 (Section 4.3) refers to a special bachelor of science degree in agriculture program for village-level workers (*gramsevaks*) conducted by an agricultural university in India. Example 3 (Section 4.4) discusses *two* instances of investment in recurrent education for women in the United States and the United Kingdom. Example 4 (Section 4.5) deals with educational programs for discharged soldiers in both the United States (under the so-called GI Bill of Rights), and the United Kingdom (under FETS, or the Further Education and Training Scheme). Example 5 (Section 4.6) concerns investment in education in the urban ghettos of the United States. Example 6 (Section 4.7) presents *two* instances of tackling the problem of unequal participation in education in the United States and France. The U.S. instance highlights the problem of underinvestment in education in rural farm areas, and the French case is that of coping with the inequalities of opportunities in the secondary school system.

Examples 1–4 are taken from Stoikov (1975, Chapter 5), Example 5 from Harrison (1972), and the cases in Example 6 from Schultz (1964) and Laderrière (1967), respectively. I should repeat here that the skeletal outlines of the investment programs are provided only to illustrate situations in which one might encounter the social-choice problems. These should not be taken, therefore, as an analysis of the actual programs.

What problems of social choice can one anticipate in these different examples? For an answer one must look at the choice situations systematically in terms of (a) the distinction between the two investment domains, both in its complementarity and its time-horizon aspects; (b) the distinction between the micro- and the macroeconomic logic of the investment decisions involved; and above all, (c) the collective-choice questions implied – in other words, the basic three arguments developed in Chapter 2. I shall bring in these arguments here in that order again in dealing with the Brazilian example in some detail. In subsequent examples, however, I stress only what appear to be the features that distinguish each case somewhat from the others.

## 4.2 Example 1: Retraining versus training (Brazil)

A number of large-scale training programs have been conducted in various countries since the 1950s with the stated objective of bridging the gap between the demand for skilled labor and the supply coming out of normal technical and vocational schools. Our example pertains to the Brazilian Intensive Program for the Preparation of Industrial Labor, which was initiated at the end of 1963.[1] I might add that available documentation does not seem to indicate any awareness, at the time of the formulation, implementation, and evaluation of the program, that there could be any social-choice dilemma in the situation.

It was estimated that Brazil's annual need for qualified labor, taking into account growth and replacement factors, was on the order of 5,000 technicians and 60,000 skilled workers. In 1963, however, the schools supplied no more than one-fifth of the estimated needs: 1,000 technicians and 12,000 skilled workers. It was argued that:

To meet the urgent needs for skilled workers and technicians, a developing nation has two training alternatives. It can train its unskilled manpower for these highly skilled occupations, or it can upgrade and retrain its semi-skilled and skilled workers. The latter is not a long-range substitute for the former, but it is a much more rapid procedure – and this is the approach followed by the Intensive Programme.[2]

The initial goal was to train, in twenty months, over 46,000 persons. After this first period, an evaluation of the program was carried out on the basis of *two* different sets of information: (a) cost data, and (b) the results of interviews with nearly 3,400 persons involved (trainees, dropouts, teachers, administrators, supervisors in employment) on their perceptions of the success or otherwise of the Program. The stated aim in analyzing the cost data was to determine what happened when the program outlay was marginally changed so as to compare the option with other available alternatives.

The evaluation study concluded that the program had served a real purpose and that its continuance was economically justified. Moreover, the program's flexibility and its ability to meet the changing labor requirements of industry were judged to be largely due to its focus on retraining.

### *Complementarity of domains*

First, consider the complementarity aspect of the distinction of the two domains of investment decisions. We have seen that societal or institutional investment can only provide the facilities required either for retraining or primary training, as the case may be, but that only individuals' own investments in time, effort, and other resources could make the facilities of any use to them. Therefore, regardless of the labor planning needs in Brazil for *providing* training of a given kind, the first operationally important question for the societal investor was whether the individuals in the target group concerned would be ready to provide the necessary complementary investments in their own domain for securing that same kind of training. It is here that the societal policymaker must watch out for the first signs of trouble. Let me suggest, for example, a possible scenario for the choice situation implicit in the Brazilian program.

Suppose that society values the retraining and upgrading of older workers employed in a given productive activity above the primary training of unskilled young entrants to the work force. The basis of this preference might itself be (though not necessarily) one simple economic calculation: It might be quicker and cheaper to train older and semiskilled workers (if they, on their part, are willing to be trained). On the other hand, the preference might be based on a value judgment made in favor of one class of individuals. But whatever the basis, this is the kind of social preference that presumably is sometimes revealed in the adoption of a scheme like the Brazilian one.

However, let us suppose further that the older workers are mostly reluctant to invest in their individual domain to secure the advantage of retraining, but that the younger workers would gladly invest their time and money to complement institutional investment in their training. Clearly, society would be forced to choose, in that case, between (a) investing in a retraining program for older workers that had a higher social priority, but in which the workers' interest in making the complementary investments is not sufficiently high, and (b) investing in a first-time training program for the young unskilled that has been assigned a lower social priority, but for which the individuals concerned are found to be ready to make the necessary investments on their part.

In the language of the standard rate-of-return approach one could perhaps describe the dilemma by saying that the impasse in complementarity arises, in this instance, because investment in retraining commands the higher marginal *social* rate of return, whereas investment in first-time training has the higher marginal *private* rate of return. Thus, it would be argued that though the former would be preferred if the social costs and benefits were to be counted, the latter would be more attractive to individuals because, obviously, they would count only their private costs and benefits.

The standard rate-of-return approach, however, would miss the crux of the societal dilemma which lies, to use the terms of the domain-distinction argument, in the juxtaposition of *two* factors. First, the private rate of return to young unskilled workers of first-time training is high enough to justify their complementary investments in the individual domain, but the private rate of return to older workers of retraining is not high enough to justify adequate investments by *them* in their own retraining. Second, society prefers the retraining of the older workers to the training of the young unskilled workers.

*Time horizons*

We come next to the time-horizon aspect of the domain-distinction argument introduced in Section 2.4. I remarked then that although individuals, by and large, had only *one* lifetime to consider when calculating the returns to their investment in education, society had before it both short-term and long-term considerations. Moreover, at any point of allocating resources for investment, the short run was, up to a point, an alternative to the long run.

To return to the Brazilian example, and if one might simplify the choice situation somewhat, although investment in the *retraining* program involved spending resources mainly on the immediate trainees, investment in programs for providing first-time training facilities would involve spending on immediate as well as future trainees, because it would include long-term investments on overheads. Schools, libraries, full-time faculty, and so on, usually provided (and possibly needed) for the young untrained will naturally have long life spans. Investments on these items, therefore, have to be judged in relatively longer and wider perspectives than those used to decide, for example, the current year's expenditure on the current year's in-service trainees. Retraining and training, differentiated in this manner, would thus be, at the margin, alternative societal investment opportunities of different time perspectives, though they might not always appear as such.

This takes one back to the consideration of the basis of the assumed social preference for retraining over training in the Brazilian example. The time-horizon aspect lets us see here that in a sense, and to a certain extent, today's societal investment in long-term facilities for the education and training of the young unskilled worker also provides a basis for *future* investments in short-term programs of retraining and upgrading skilled and semiskilled older workers of tomorrow. One thereby perceives how there could arise an element of contradiction in the societal judgment involved, for example, in a decision to diminish investment in long-term facilities for training the young in order to provide for more short-term retraining schemes for older workers. The contradiction could arise, first, because today's young workers would be tomorrow's veterans. They would need, hopefully, fewer investments in retraining or upgrading tomorrow if they are trained today. Second, and perhaps more definitely, the long-term facilities created today are not only for today: They would be available also for the short-term programs of tomorrow.

The social-choice dilemma foreshadowed by the time-horizon aspect is not apparent at the formulation stage of the Brazilian program for one obvious reason. The assumption at that stage is that retraining is only a temporary expediency. It is part of a crash program embarked upon to meet a short-term supply difficulty, a "bottleneck," to be discontinued as soon as the excess demand in the labor market for highly qualified personnel is met. Presumably it is anticipated that once the excess demand disappears, the system would be left to revert to the normal processes of the market equating supply with demand through the regular production of graduates in existing vocational and technical schools. In real life, however, what at first appears to be only a temporary bottleneck is not always indubitably so – it is not always a passing phenomenon. Nor could the information supplied in the example automatically reassure one that it was indeed so in the case of Brazil.

In fact, the shortage of skilled labor perceived relative to the needs of Brazil's developing economy may not have been entirely casual, or even cyclical, in the way such shortages often can be in a developed economy. Therefore, the societal investment decision in the retraining and upgrading of personnel in Brazil is not necessarily insulated from other more long-term investment decisions in education and training on the grounds that it is purely ad hoc, and the circumstances supporting it are unlikely to continue indefinitely. If the observed excess demand for skilled personnel does continue for any length of time, then the retraining and upgrading program would probably have solved one short-term problem of supplying skills at the cost of *aggravating* the problem in the long run.

There can be no simple answer as to where and how society should strike a balance between the two types of investment. Society must respond to the current demand for retraining and must take into account whatever complementary investment decisions are made in the individual domain by older workers. But society must also consider the expected demand for education and training over a long period and into the future, taking into account the expected investment decisions of those who would be the uninitiated young trainees at successive moments in time.

Taking aspects of complementarity and the time horizon together, the domain-distinction argument raises a question that requires the societal investor to consider what is expected to happen in the Brazilian economy over time with regard to the excess demand for skilled personnel. It is at this stage that the micro–macro distinction might usefully be brought in.

### *Macroeconomic considerations*

Let us look at the alternatives before the societal investor purely from the standpoint of clearing the excess demand for skilled labor in the Brazilian labor market. Suppose that the alternatives are (a) investment in the short-term program of retraining for older skilled and semiskilled persons; (b) investment in a long-term program of education and training for young people through expanding the existing capacity of the schooling system; and (c) a mixed program of investments in retraining as well as training. The question then is: What are the macroeconomic considerations for arriving at the correct mix of investments in this case? It may be recalled from the discussion in Section 2.5 that two considerations would be involved here. First, the societal investor must try to determine the impact of the aggregate investment contemplated in retraining and training on the market. Second, one must allow for the difference between the logic of the macroeconomic state of expectations in the market, and the equally valid logic of individuals' microlevel expectations. We saw that individuals had greater justification for investing in their own domain on the basis of current market information than society had on both counts: (a) Society could not take that information as a parameter because it had to consider relatively large aggregate investments; and (b) society could not evaluate social returns in the aggregate in the presence of the uncertainty of employment for individuals in the same way that individuals could in calculating their own prospects.

In the Brazilian case, too, the societal investor must be wary of the possibility of coming up against the resulting dilemma. To return to our scenario, let us assume that the *reason* why society preferred investment in retraining to primary training was precisely the macroeconomic consideration that either (a) large investments in increasing the capacity for imparting education and training in the schools would depress the returns to skill formation, or (b) continued investment in primary training eventually would create some aggregate unemployment among skilled personnel. It is clear that in either case individuals would be equally justified in pressing for their primary training, each individual concerned being ready to pay the necessary price for the prospect – if not the certainty – of higher returns.

### *Social-choice problems*

Let me now enumerate the choice dilemmas that the foregoing discussion presents the societal investor in Brazilian education. First is the dilemma of complementarity of domains: Society prefers the outcome of investment in *A* to the outcome of investment in *B*, but for each needs adequate complementary investments by the individuals concerned. However, the individuals concerned in *B* are ready to invest adequately, but those concerned in *A* are not. Second is the complicated dilemma of time horizons: Society prefers the short-term outcome of investment in *A* to the short-term outcome of investment in *B*, but not to the long-term outcome of investment in *B*, because investment in *B* is necessary *today* for the investment in *A* to be feasible *tomorrow*.

Third is the dilemma of micro–macro logic: Society prefers investment in *A* to investment in *B* on the basis of (correct) expectations of the impact on the market of the aggregate of investments over a chosen period of time. However, individuals prefer investment in *B* to investment in *A* on the basis of their (also correct) individual expectations as to the impact of their investment decision in their lifetime and on their prospects.

Two conclusions would seem to follow from our analysis of the categories of social-choice dilemmas in judging instances of institutional investment in education. Though these are made in the specific context of the Brazilian example, they would apply equally to the others cited later in this chapter. Stating these conclusions here, therefore, might add to the clarity of the following sections in addition to making it easier to avoid repetitious analysis of each example.

First, and quite obviously, though the dilemmas analyzed differ widely – and one could also expect specific variations within each category in the different real-life examples – they have an interesting common feature: They emerge, as was shown in Section 2.6, only because either the domain-distinction or the macroeconomic argument had failed at some point to provide society with an unambiguous investment criterion. It is precisely at that point that the collective-choice argument has to be brought in for further clarification of the issues.

Second, when all the information on the three types of dilemmas has come in, and all the considerations of the domain-distinction and the micro–macro argument are before society, two questions would remain for societal judgment: (a) how to combine, or decide between, the conflicting interests of different (groups of) individuals, some of them even belonging to future generations; and (b) how to combine, or decide between, the conflicting judgments of different individuals on what constitutes the best interest of all.

Essentially, whether the next societal investment in education is to be in a retraining program or in a program involving, say, an increased number of school places is not a question that is really being asked about the same set of persons. The question would have different meanings for different persons because, in the first place, their interests would not be the same. By *interests* I mean individual interests of the persons to be educated, which would determine their individual preferences and thereby their microlevel investment decisions in education in the individual domain. Furthermore, besides pure self-interest, individuals also carry their own sets of judgments about what ought to be done in the collective interest. Young entrants to the work force as well as older workers would have their own individual views about the right ordering of societal investments in education that may or may not be the same as the order individuals reveal in their own investment decisions.

The collective-choice argument, therefore, ultimately concerns social choice in situations where individuals can have both different interests in the outcomes of investment in education *and* different judgments about the resultant collective good. The correct mix of investments in education for different sets of people, in the final analysis, cannot be decided on the presumption that there is, as it were, only *one* representative individual for society to be concerned about. This is the common theme of the lessons to be drawn from all the examples of the social-choice dilemma in societal investments in education.

## 4.3 Example 2: Bachelor of science course for village-level workers (India)

The link between village-level developmental work in India and the national effort in planning and implementation is sustained through a well-defined formal network. The districts within every state in India have been subdivided into developmental blocks, each of which is headed by a block development officer (BDO). The blocks are further divided into village groups, each group comprising ten or so villages. The village-level development officer is the *gramsevak* (literally, servant of the village), who is the formal link between the BDO and the village group.

With the sharp shift in agricultural technology in the mid-1960s, particularly associated with the introduction of new techniques of cultivation with high-yielding varieties of seeds, there had to be a corresponding increase in the level of expertise required of the *gramsevaks*. They now needed to understand and be able to explain the fairly complex input characteristics of the new hybrid seeds in terms of the use of modern pesticides, chemical fertilizers, and sophisticated water control. In 1961, a special degree program was introduced in an Indian agricultural university that permitted *gramsevaks* to qualify for the bachelor of science degree in agriculture in two years instead of the normal three.[3] In allowing a one-year reduction in the length of formal schooling, the university was recognizing the experience of the field worker in agricultural extension work as a substitute for a year's stay in college.

The results of the program have been analyzed from the standpoint of efficiency and equity by Richard Shortlidge as reported in Stoikov (1975).[4] Shortlidge's evaluation is based on answers to *two* questions: (1) Have the resources invested in the special program for the *gramsevaks* given as high a rate of return as those invested in the regular degree program? (2) Has the special program been successful in extending higher education to a lower socioeconomic group?

To answer the first question, the average social rates of return were calculated by following standard procedures discussed in the preceding chapter. The calculations were made for *gramsevaks* taking the degree in agriculture and for the regular graduates who had found employment in government service after obtaining their bachelor of science degree in agriculture. The study found that the social rate of return for the *gramsevaks* was 13.5% against 9.9% for the regular graduates, assuming that both groups generated the same social benefits as measured by the actual gains in the earnings of the regular graduates. However, if the social benefits of the *gramsevaks* were to be measured by the actual gains in their earnings through promotion in service, then the average social rate of return for the *gramsevaks* fell to a mere 8.3%.[5]

As to the second question, which concerns equity, the study found that among the regular undergraduates the median landholding was thirty acres. This places them in the top 1% socioeconomic group of rural India. On the other hand, the mean landholding for the *gramsevaks* lay between ten and fifteen acres, which places them among approximately the top 10% of India's landholding families. The conclusion, therefore, is that the special program allows the participation of a poorer socioeconomic group, though not one of the poorest in India.

### *Social-choice problems*

What types of social choice problems could be expected to arise in this case? It may be interesting to note that although both the setting and the specifications of the choice situation here are vastly different from those in Example 1, some of the basic considerations are remarkably similar. Take, for instance, the aspect of complementarity of the two domains of investment decisions. In the Indian example, as in the Brazilian one, there emerges the possibility of a societal dilemma, and in fact, in the Indian case, there is an additional complication. The fact that the *gramsevaks* gain rather less on graduation, by way of increased earnings if they decide to stick to their jobs, compared to the regular agriculture graduate in government service, can have two consequences for the complementarity of investments. First, it is conceivable, in the circumstances described, that the investments in the individual domain would be forthcoming less enthusiastically from the *gramsevaks* in the special program meant for them, than from the regular students in the normal agriculture course. At the same time, society might continue to prefer the outcome of investment in the special program to the outcome of an investment in the regular course. This is a direct dilemma of complementarity of domains of exactly the same type as we observed in Example 1.

Example 2, however, exhibits a second, additional feature that could lead to what may be called an indirect dilemma. It is conceivable, for example, that the *gramsevaks* would find it profitable to accept the special program, but having invested in it, to then seek the (presumably) higher earnings of the college graduate and move away from their original jobs. This would imply that the societal investment based on the anticipated social benefits of the *gramsevaks'* knowledge of the technology of the high-yielding seed varieties would prove to have been largely in vain. In other words, the presumed complementary investments in the individual domain would turn out to have been not complementary after all. This is a feature of the complementarity problem that can provide an interesting variation of "brain drain" within, and out of, many developing economies with imperfect labor markets.

Turning now to the time-horizon aspect, one would find that the dilemma in this case, assuming that the special program for the *gramsevaks* required only short-term investments or at least smaller long-term investments than the regular university program, is similar to that in Example 1. It is therefore unnecessary to repeat the same argument here.

So far as the dilemma of the micro–macro points of view is concerned, the main considerations are again broadly similar to what we encountered in Example 1. Society might want lower investment in the regular bachelor of science degree in agriculture program and higher investment in the special program for the *gramsevaks* already employed, with the macroeconomic expectation that soon there would be no new jobs for the fresh agriculture graduates. On the other hand, individuals planning to invest in a regular college education in agriculture for themselves might nevertheless be equally justified in deciding to face a calculated risk of unemployment, because, for them, the prospects, even after allowing fully for that risk, might still be very attractive. It may be recalled that precisely this consequence of the distinction between individuals' uncertainty at the microlevel and the uncertainty (or rather the lack of it) for the economy at the macrolevel was discussed in Section 2.5.

The three possible social-choice dilemmas suggested in this example arise, as in Example 1, from a similar, though not the same, set of considerations involving complementarity and the time-horizon aspects of domain distinction, and the micro–macro logic of uncertainty about the labor market. What is important to note in these three instances is that the real choice forced upon society in each case is between the interests of two different sets of individuals in circumstances in which it is by no means given that interpersonal comparisons between them are permissible.

How different the two sets of individuals are is indeed what the *second* question in the evaluation by Shortlidge seeks to establish. That the answer seems to place one set (the regular students of the agricultural university) socioeconomically in the top 1% and the other set (the *gramsevaks*) only in the top 10% of the population might indeed sound warning bells for the societal decision maker. Whereas Example 1 demonstrated intergenerational comparability of welfare, the present one involves welfare comparison between two economic (and social) groups, one presumably disadvantaged relative to the other.

## 4.4 Example 3: Investment in women's education for reentry (United Kingdom, United States)

Recurrent education for women must continue as a separate theme for societal concern so long as the withdrawal of women from the labor force for long periods of time is a dominant mode in the labor market.[6] Since World War II, the developed countries have witnessed a tremendous expansion in the proportion of women working outside the home. Even in developing countries the recent expansion of the educational and health sectors of the economies has brought about an abrupt and substantial increase in the demand for skilled and trained women in the labor force. Traditionally, the increased supply comes from among women in the post-childbearing ages and the immediate posteducational and premarital years. The choice at the margin, therefore, is often between spending additional societal resources on secondary and higher education of "regular" students (men as well as women) and spending on education and training specifically with a view to helping women reenter the work force after a period of withdrawal during childbearing and childrearing years.

There have been a number of recurrent or continuing education programs for women in the United Kingdom and the United States that have attracted sufficiently large public or societal investments and involved wide enough participation by women to justify careful analysis of the problems of social choice posed by these programs. The Open University[7] in the United Kingdom, for example, provides some interesting evidence along this line as do the continuing education programs of the University of Pittsburgh and other centers in the United States.[8] The evidence suggests that the Open University in the United Kingdom attracts older women primarily in the post-childrearing ages. They also tend to come from the more affluent socioeconomic groups. An interesting fact about the University of Pittsburgh experience is that a high proportion of women who had failed to complete their baccalaureate degree returned when the continuing education program was introduced.

Yet, despite these and other education programs for older age-groups, the experience is that there is some reluctance on the part of women to participate in them. Stoikov (1975, p. 71) attributes this to the fact that these programs generally offer only a traditional form of higher education. Long absence from the environment of formal learning and the predominance of younger people as a competing group possibly add uncertainty to older women's decision to return to school. The evidence that they prefer short training courses in vocational areas may be a reflection of this uncertainty.

Furthermore, Stoikov points out, admission standards in regular universities, which are open to older students, are geared to the performance abilities of young people fresh from secondary school. The experience and performance of older women in the community and in the home are seldom taken into account for meeting the admission requirements of a regular four-year institution. On the other hand, short-cycle educational schemes, such as the community colleges in the United States, which cater to disadvantaged groups (including older women), unfortunately face problems of good-quality staff recruitment and of status in the community.[9] What implications do these considerations have for the societal investment in education programs for the reentry of women into the work force?

### *Social-choice problems*

Perhaps I need not elaborate again the points brought out in the previous examples but only reiterate that, in this case, too many of the considerations are broadly similar. For example, the two aspects of the domain-distinction argument (i.e., the complementarity of investments and the variety of time horizons) both need to be considered carefully before deciding on making new investments in institutions such as the community colleges. Similarly, one must try to assess the quantitative impact of the aggregate of estimated investments in recurrent education for women in the institutional as well as the individual domains on the future earnings of both women *and* men. One must also take into account the possibility of sharp differences between micro- and macrolevel expectations leading to conflicting investment decisions in the individual and the institutional domains. All these situations are discussed in the previous examples.

Finally, the familiar social-choice problem reappears in the shape of a conflict of interests of judgments between different sets of individuals, such as older women seeking to reenter the work force and young entrants – men and women. One could, of course, think of other sets of individuals' being similarly involved in this question.

Although one need not anticipate which of these various considerations would appear more crucial in the actual circumstances when all the facts are assembled, there is at least one interesting distinguishing feature of the present example that needs to be brought out. This involves the nature of the complementarity aspect of domain distinction, which is brought out in this case in a basically different form. For contrast, let me recall the problem of complementarity as it arose in Examples 1 and 2. In the first example, the question was whether the older workers of Brazil would find their retraining program sufficiently attractive in terms of upgrading themselves to justify the extra expense and effort called for on their part. In the second example, there arose a similar question: Would the *gramsevaks* of India find a bachelor of science course in agriculture sufficiently attractive in terms of the investments in time and effort required of them and their earnings prospects? In both cases, it may be noted, the uncertainty or doubts, if any, of the individuals concerned their private returns to the individual investments and not the form of the investment itself. In other words, there appear to be no grounds for suspecting, on the basis of the evidence, that the investment itself might be inappropriate in the sense that it might not add sufficiently to productivity from the social point of view. In both cases the assumption rather is that society finds the investment worthwhile, and the question remains whether the individuals concerned also do.

In the case of the return of older women to education, however, there is no such assurance as the evidence from the Open University in the United Kingdom or of the community colleges in the United States would seem to suggest. Here individuals may sometimes be called upon to invest on terms that are often quite discouraging – comparatively to competing groups of individuals – in some of the aspects of the schooling, though not necessarily in terms of the expected returns. The observed reluctance to come forward with complementary investment in the individual domain arises here, therefore, for other reasons ("Performance requirements favor the agility of youth rather than the experience of age," for example) rather than as a result of insufficient prospects of increased earnings in a direct sense.

The operational implications of the two types of deficiency in complementary investment in the individual domain would obviously also be quite different. With regard to reentry, one could seek ways to change the form of the institutional investment itself for providing more suitable means of recognizing and developing the skills of older women. On the other hand, in the other cases one could see whether a larger part of the increase in the social product brought about by the investment concerned could not be passed on to those individuals who were to make the complementary investments in the individual domain in the first place.

## 4.5 Example 4: Education of veterans (United Kingdom, United States)

Investments in education for the reintegration of the discharged soldier into the civilian labor force attained massive proportions in several countries as World War II ended.[10] In the United States the bulk of the educational benefits for veterans was administered under the so-called GI Bill of Rights (PL 346 – the Serviceman's Adjustment Act of 1944).[11] In the United Kingdom it was the Further Education and Training Scheme (FETS), which covered an even larger segment of the population than the American program in that it included everybody who had done work recognized as of "national importance."

Belying fears that the ex-servicemen's educational benefit programs would turn the university experience into "a form of cheapened impractical vocational experience," in fact, there was no significant difference in academic performance between veterans and regular college students in the United States.[12] Similarly, in the United Kingdom an unusually large percentage of the FETS trainees completed the programs successfully.[13]

Studies suggested that investments in separate programs for the veterans succeeded mainly when the special features of their reentry problem were taken into account. Since most of these features would be expected to be also present whenever a large body of relatively older workers have to be retrained through massive reintegration programs, it is not surprising that the progress of the educational schemes for veterans in the United States has positively influenced the development of recurrent education all over the world.

### *Social-choice problems*

The following characteristics, listed by Loring and Anderson (1971), as cited in Stoikov (1975), show why societal investors in the education of veterans should consider this group as distinct from regular students in many respects, apart from obviously being older. This would suggest how serious the problem of interpersonal comparability could be between the two groups of individuals for calculating the social benefits of educating them.

Loring and Anderson (1971) listed ten characteristics that they considered important among those that seemed to be associated with the American ex-serviceman. These, they suggested, should be borne in mind when designing recurrent education programs for veterans. These characteristics are particularly worth noting because many, if not all, of them are also likely to apply to "veterans" in the nonmilitary sense, that is, older workers in general: (1) high individual motivation; (2) anxiety at being above average age; (3) desire to be respected for past experience; (4) modest academic self-concept; (5) diversity of verbal skill levels; (6) ambivalence toward authority; (7) general sense of discipline; (8) lack of career plans; (9) dissatisfaction with the "establishment"; and (10) need for considerable readjustment.

Some of these characteristics would be determined primarily by the individual's self-interest and others by what I would call the level of individual judgments. As Stoikov (1975) observes pertinently in this context:

> New social situations, however, place new demands on these recurrent education schemes. Fendrich, for example, points out that the Black veteran from Viet-Nam is torn between the United States' two great traumas: the war itself and racial tension.[14] Any veterans' benefit scheme must take account of these new specific needs of the Black veteran.

In much the same vein this also can be said of the prospects for similar recurrent education plans in other countries: In India, for example, these plans must take into account the great traumas caused by caste, linguistic, and regional divisions.

Social-choice problems, therefore, can be seen to emerge not only where individual interests are incompatible or judgments differ from individual to individual – basically the setting for the societal dilemmas described in the earlier examples. They also occur when the judgment of the same individual is found to be split, in a certain sense. Over and above the considerations that come to the fore in the discussion of the previous examples there is, then, one more that emerges rather interestingly in this case. This consideration also has to do with translating individual preferences into the preferences of society, but there is an important difference. In the other examples discussed so far, one finds that the dilemma arises at the level of collective choice either because the individual *interests* can conflict (the old vs. the young, the poor vs. the rich, etc.), or because the collection of the individuals' interests can conflict with their *collective* judgment (micro- vs. macrolevel logic).

The present example, however, exposes another possible societal dilemma in which individuals' *own* value judgments pull them in different directions and their thinking has to be seen as that of either splintered or composite and many-faceted personalities. The present example, therefore, points out an additional complication in making societal investment decisions in education involving groups or individuals who are more complexly motivated than those encountered in conventional choice theory.

## 4.6 Example 5: Unequal returns to human capital (United States)

Bennett Harrison (1972) made an interesting study of the benefits accruing to ghetto dwellers in American cities from investments in education.[15] His sample covered over 37,000 individuals from records collected by the U.S. Department of Labor for the year 1966. The following is a summary of the main results showing how differently the same kinds of investments in education affected two different groups of ghetto dwellers: blacks and whites. It is necessary to remember here that this is not the full story of the discrimination encountered, because no account is given of the differential rewards of education between the ghetto dwellers and the rest of the urban population.

The weekly wage of white high school graduates in a pooled set of twelve poverty areas is nearly $25 higher than that of whites who never attended high school. For nonwhites, the difference is only \$8.33. High school, therefore, has three times as high a marginal payoff for ghetto whites as for ghetto nonwhites. On the assumptions of a forty-year working life, a rectangular lifetime earnings distribution, and a 6% rate of time preference, the present value of lifetime return to completion of high school is calculated to be nearly \$19,000 for whites, but only \$6,000 for nonwhites.

For whites, the risk of unemployment falls with years of school completed. Over the interval nine to twelve years inclusive, the expectation of joblessness falls by 4.0%. For white college graduates it falls an additional 1.9%. For nonwhites, on the other hand, the average effect of education on unemployment, though statistically significant, is found to be numerically small. A white college graduate from the slums can expect to be out of work involuntarily nearly three weeks less per year than a white high school dropout who also lives in one of the urban ghettos in the sample. But nonwhites have only a 0.7% lower risk of unemployment than high school dropouts if they have graduated, and that effect ends with the high school diploma though 8.3% of the nonwhite ghetto sample completed at least some college.

On the basis of the study, Harrison concludes that education facilitates entry of both white and nonwhite ghetto workers into new occupations and, at least for whites, leads to greater interoccupational mobility. But once there, nonwhites find themselves *underemployed* again, receiving earnings that are hardly above the levels enjoyed in the previous position and facing the same expectations of being unemployed. For ghetto whites, on the other hand, the occupational mobility facilitated by education is translated into substantially higher earnings and significantly lower risks of joblessness.

### *Social-choice problems*

I will not dwell again on the considerations here that have been discussed in the previous examples, important as they are. Societal investment policy in education in a depressed area would have to consider many of the problems of choice that have been brought out in the other examples. Let me therefore confine the discussion here to one aspect of investment policy for society that was not prominent in any of the other examples. I refer to the inequality of job opportunities between groups on whom the same societal investments in education have been made. I may explain this by briefly recalling the previous examples.

In Example 1, the question presumably does not arise because (in the short run) the assumption is one of great shortage of skilled labor in Brazil. In Example 2, I assume that the *gramsevaks* of India, if they leave their original jobs on receiving the bachelor of science degree, *would* be able to compete on equal terms with regular college graduates. I assume this – though with misgivings, since the latter are found to belong to a distinctly higher socioeconomic group – because the example presents no obvious evidence to the contrary. In Example 3, I again assume, for the same reason, that if the older women who want to reenter the labor market manage to enter and graduate from the school, which seems to favor younger groups, then the labor market would not practice further discrimination against them. In Example 4, a similar assumption is made, perhaps with greater justification, about the job opportunities of trained ex-servicemen.

Discussing policy recommendations, Harrison quotes Michelson (1969): "Equal education should be a goal in itself, not diminished for its failure to produce income for non-whites."[16] and recommends a number of special measures for blacks. It is interesting to note that the finding of unequal rewards of education does not necessarily lead to the judgment that investable resources should be shifted from groups that earn lower returns, to groups that earn higher returns from educational investments. This would be following the rule of optimization, assuming absolute interpersonal comparability. On the contrary, as in the present example, it may lead to the social judgment that the observed unequal rewards were unjustified and, therefore, compensatory investment policy was now indicated in the form of *greater* allocation of funds to the education of those whose ability to reap the advantages of education was found so undeservedly low.

## 4.7 Example 6: Inequality of educational opportunity (United States, France)

If the preceding example highlighted the problem of societal decision making in educational investments when the returns were judged to be *undeservedly* unequal, the present example (comprising two illustrations from two countries) exposes inequality or inequity at another, earlier point: that of responding to the available opportunity to invest in education. Schultz (1964) provides evidence of this kind of inequality in rural farm areas of the United States, and Laderrière (1967) presents an extensive report on the inequalities in the French educational system as a whole.[17] In the latter example, for the sake of brevity, I shall confine myself to the inequalities of opportunity only in the secondary education system (as of 1961–2).

Schultz (1964) brings out clearly the extreme unevenness of education among white and nonwhite workers in rural and urban areas in the United States over the period 1940–62. Participation in higher education over this period is found to be significantly lower than average in the rural areas, particularly in the southern states. College enrollment in 1960 indicated that 48% of urban high school graduates attended college, whereas only 32% of rural high school graduates continue their education. Schultz's hypothesis is that these differences followed from the difference in the quality of education imparted in the respective areas.[18] For example, he would argue that there was underinvestment in education in poorer states and in rural areas because farm people generally lacked the means, the necessary information, and therefore the incentive to make untried investment decisions on the quantity and quality of further schooling that might be available for themselves or their children. A relatively low-quality primary education prevented them from making what could have turned out to be the correct optimum investment decisions concerning further education.

That the market or the economy may not automatically provide equal opportunities for investment in education has, of course, been accepted as a well-known fact of life for educational planning in a number of countries. Laderrière (1967) has reported extensively on different types of inequalities of opportunity in French education. The synoptic account given here is based on that report but is limited, as I have mentioned, to the information pertaining to secondary education.

*Three* types of inequality in participation in secondary education in France may be noted. As reflected in Tables 4.1–4.3, one observes *regional* inequalities in the rate of entry, inequalities in the rate of entry between socioeconomic groups, and inequality in terms of a third index: access to the more prestigious *lycée* rather than the *Collège d'enseignement général* (CEG). The rate of entry into the system is considered to be particularly useful for determining how

Table 4.1. *Percentage of pupils 11 to 12 years old entering general secondary education according to population of area of residence*

| Area of residence | *Collèges d'enseignement général*[a] | *Lycées* | Total for 6th |
|---|---|---|---|
| Rural cantons | 28 | 14 | 42 |
| Less than 5,000 inhabitants | 40 | 18 | 58 |
| 5,000 to 10,000 inhabitants | 38 | 19 | 57 |
| 10,000 to 50,000 inhabitants | 25 | 42 | 67 |
| 50,000 to 200,000 inhabitants | 17 | 46 | 63 |
| More than 200,000 inhabitants | 22 | 42 | 64 |
| Paris conurbation | 39 | 33 | 72 |
| Total | 28 | 27 | 55 |

[a] The *collège d'enseignement général* is a school in the first cycle of general secondary education; during the first four years of general secondary education, it has the so-called short curriculum of the same level as the "modern" sections of the traditional *lycées*. Some *collèges* also have a curriculum on the lines of the classical section; in contrast to the traditional lycées, the teaching staff consists of primary teachers who have had, for the most part, special training. The creation of comprehensive schools in the first cycle, which are intended to receive all pupils after completion of their five years of primary education, resulted in a modification of the structure of *collèges d'enseignement général*.

*Source*: A. Girard, H. Bastide, G. Pourcher, "Enquète Nationale sur l'entrée en sixième et la démocratisation de l'enseignement," *Population*, January–March 1963, No. 1.

much has been done to seek out aptitudes. This rate is calculated from the ratio of the total number of pupils in the "6th" (first year of secondary education: eleven to twelve years of age) to the total number in the second year of the *cours moyen* during the preceding school years (representing the fifth year of primary education: ten to eleven years of age). Table 4.1 (last column) shows the relationship between the population of the area of residence (and thus the extent of urbanization) and the rate of entry into the 6th. Table 4.2 (last column) similarly relates parental socioeconomic category to the rate of entry.

Finally, Table 4.3 (which also includes figures for students at universities) shows the correspondence between parental background and the *types* of educational institutions the pupils attended. It may be noted that in the context of the French educational system the CEG, the more modest institution compared to the lycée, is also usually located in a rural area and is attended by pupils from lower

Table 4.2. *Percentage of pupils 11 to 12 years old entering general secondary education according to parental background*

| Occupations of parents | *Collèges d'enseignement général* | *Lycée* | Total in 6th |
|---|---|---|---|
| None and undefined | 23 | 14 | 37 |
| Farm workers | 21 | 11 | 32 |
| Farm owners | 24 | 16 | 40 |
| Industrial workers | 29 | 16 | 45 |
| Artisans and retail merchants | 34 | 32 | 66 |
| Office workers | 34 | 33 | 67 |
| Middle-level personnel | 29 | 55 | 84 |
| Liberal professions | 23 | 67 | 90 |
| Top-level personnel | 19 | 75 | 94 |
| Total | 28 | 27 | 55 |

*Source*: See Table 4.1.

income categories. Table 4.3, therefore, provides an additional indicator of inequality in French education.

### *Social-choice problems*

What *additional* implications, apart from those discussed in the earlier examples, can the perception of inequality of educational opportunities have for societal investment policy? Let me briefly go back to the two illustrations in this example. In the first, Schultz judges the quality of (presumably elementary) education imparted in rural areas of the United States to be comparatively deficient, which therefore accounts for the fact that rural workers do not see the advantage of further education as much as they should, or as much as urban workers do. An alternative judgment could be that individual investments in further education were not forthcoming because the education offered was not good enough. In either case, the remedy would be what might be called reverse discrimination in societal investment policy: Favor more investments in (improving the quality of) education in the rural area than in the urban area.

The dilemma for societal investors, however, is that the nature of the remedy here depends solely on their judgment that the *quality* of education in the rural area was, in some way, to blame. But the judgment, in principle, could also be that the urban workers in-

Table 4.3. *Social background of secondary school pupils and students at universities, 1961–2 (%)*

| Type of school | Farm owners | Farm workers | Heads of commercial or industrial enterprises: Industry | Com-merce | Crafts | Liberal profes-sions and top level person-nel | Middle-level person-nel | Employ-ees in industry and commerce | Industri-al worker | House-hold help | Persons without occupa-tion | Other | Total |
|---|---|---|---|---|---|---|---|---|---|---|---|---|---|
| Classical and modern *lycées* [a] | 6.5 | 1.2 | 2.1 | 9.2 | 5.3 | 17.1 | 15.9 | 17.0 | 15.9 | 1.2 | 2.5 | 6.1 | 100 |
| Technical (vocational) *lycées* and similar institutions | 6.0 | 1.7 | 1.7 | 7.4 | 6.1 | 5.7 | 11.1 | 17.4 | 32.5 | 2.0 | 3.4 | 5.0 | 100 |
| *Collèges d'enseignement général* | 10.0 | 2.7 | 0.8 | 7.4 | 6.3 | 2.4 | 10.6 | 16.7 | 35.0 | 1.8 | 1.8 | 4.5 | 100 |
| *Collèges d'enseignement technique* | 6.0 | 3.9 | 0.5 | 3.8 | 4.6 | 1.4 | 5.6 | 11.9 | 49.9 | 3.1 | 3.9 | 5.4 | 100 |
| Higher education in universities (facultіes) | 5.6 | 0.6 | 4.0 | 9.7 | 3.9 | 28.5 | 17.8 | 8.0 | 6.4 | 0.9 | 7.0 | 7.6 | 100 |
| Percentage of total active population (1962) | 15.7 | 4.3 | | 10.4 | | 4.0 | 7.8 | 12.6 | 36.7 | 5.4 | 3.1 | | 100 |

[a] Excluding students in classes preparing for the *Grandes Ecoles*.
*Source*: *Informations statistiques*, no. 60–61, June–July 1964.

vested more in their education for no other reason than that they were, in fact, more interested in investing in education than rural workers. This – what I might loosely call the judgment of the market – would point to the urban area where, complementary investments in the individual domain being abundant, societal investments in education should also go.

I need not elaborate further on the point that there is always a dilemma involved in "reverse discrimination." If farm workers do not want to go to college whereas urban workers do, then society might decide to invest more in providing for the farm workers' college education to make it more worthwhile for them to spend their resources in securing it. On the other hand, society might decide to invest more on providing for urban workers' college education since they are keen to invest in their own domain to secure it.

Let me now turn to the inequalities of educational opportunities in the French system. It is easy to see that the type of dilemma I refer to in the U.S. example could be present here, too. For example, if children from the poorer socioeconomic group fail to find their way to the lycée then one of two things might have happened. It might be that their superior talents remained undiscovered or unappreciated, to the detriment of societal efficiency. On the other hand, it might also be that their failure had come about merely because their motivation was too poor or their innate ability was not up to the mark. How, then, would society decide whether to invest more on the child who does not get into the lycée, or on the one who does, presumably on merit, albeit coming from a higher income group? If societal investors decide for reasons of efficiency alone, they would still have to examine why the child does not mak it to the lycée. If, in addition, the goal of equality is set forth as a equity consideration in its own right, then society is in a prope equity–efficiency "quandary."[19] Then, even the knowledge tha poorer children are being ruled out on merit would not necessari rule out a societal decision to invest more in their education t cushion the social effects of a double deprivation.

Finally, let me conclude by touching upon another difficult aspe of the social-choice problem in educational investment that th French illustration should immediately warn us of. It is present the familiar index-number problem whenever we bring in mo than one indicator of inequality or disadvantage on which to ba our compensatory social policy. We see in Table 4.1, for example, that there is a great disparity in the rates of entry into secondary education between pupils living in rural cantons (42%) and pupils living in towns of 10,000 inhabitants and over ( at least 63%). Again, Table 4.2 shows a similar disparity between the rates of entry into secondary education of children of farm workers (32%) and industrial workers (45%). It is also evident from the two tables that the rate of entry for the children of farm workers is, not unexpectedly, below the average for the rural cantons, and similarly, the rate of entry for the children of industrial workers is below the average for the towns.

The social-choice question that arises here is how to determine the relative weights of the two inequalities: between the rural area and the towns, and between the workers and the more advantaged socioeconomic groupings. It may well be that promoting educational investments in the rural sector might increase the inequality of educational opportunity between the rich and the poor. A policy of providing greater educational facilities for industrial workers, however, might increase the inequality of educational opportunity between the urban and the rural poor. Clearly, in situations where the indicators of inequality of opportunity are not two, but many (between sexes, classes, religions, castes, and regions), the possibility of the societal dilemma's emerging is also increased many times.

CHAPTER 5

# Social-choice dilemmas in education

## 5.1 Choice situations and choice dilemmas

The examples presented in Chapter 4 not only described the six different choice situations but also brought out more than six choice dilemmas that these situations entailed for societal investors in education. What might appear, at first sight, as remarkable about each one of these examples is its apparent uniqueness. Each seems to have its own interesting point of departure and each seems also to represent one particular type of social-choice problem rather more than any other. However, it must be realized that this apparent and plausible correspondence of a chosen example to a particular choice dilemma, which is emphasized in its description, is often fortuitous – depending largely on how the sequence of examples has been presented. Although the uniqueness of the choice situation encountered in each instance is certainly to be remarked upon, the analysis in Chapter 4, it should be recalled, stresses only the additional choice problems when a new example is introduced. This no doubt avoids a repetitious discussion of the features of a given example that had been already noted in preceding ones. But then, the problem singled out for special treatment in a given example also stands out, and this might indeed blur a large common ground that often exists *between* the different examples.

Each of the examples, in other words, may carry with it a whole package of social-choice problems even though only one or two may be emphasized in each new example, depending on how a given sequence of examples is taken up. This, briefly, may be taken as the justification for addressing this concluding chapter to the question of a classification of the types of social-choice dilemmas that might arise in investment in education over the entire range of the examples, rather than of the social-choice situations themselves represented in the selected examples.[1]

If we examine all the social-choice dilemmas that one comes

across in the examples in Chapter 4, as I shall presently do, it should be clear that they arise broadly in two easily distinguishable ways. First, a social-choice problem may be present by *implication*, as some paradoxical choice situation is uncovered by either the domain-distinction or the micro–macro argument. As I suggested in Chapter 2 (Sections 2.3 and 2.6), the social-choice argument comes to the fore when either of the other two arguments breaks down in the sense of producing contradictory signals for societal investment decisions. It is at such points that some basic incompatibility of individual preferences or judgments can be seen to have been implicated. However, the social-choice dilemmas that may arise in this way need not be seen as such, or as matters of anyone's direct concern, by the societal investor.

Society, for example, might be only immediately or directly concerned with a disequilibrium problem. This may originate in the choice of short- and long-term investment projects in education because of the time-horizon aspect, or it may develop due to the impact of aggregate investments in education on inflation or the level of unemployment. But then, while pursuing some of these direct equilibrium concerns of society one might encounter a paradoxical choice situation. That would then indicate *indirectly* that here lurked a genuine social-choice problem. Examples 1–4 in Chapter 4 provide illustrations of social-choice problems of this kind. The dilemmas here can be deduced from situations that could be described at least as potentially disequilibrating, if not openly so, in the ordinary sense of the market. Whether or not they are also actually and directly perceived by societal decision makers as dilemmas, that is, as situations of conflicting individual preferences and judgments, is, of course, another matter.

Social-choice problems also may be recognized explicitly and without the attendant observed or anticipated disequilibrium in the market. In the example in which it was found that exactly the same kinds of investments in education have led to different kinds of rewards for different groups of people, society might feel directly concerned with the equity aspect of the question and consider an appropriate remedial investment policy. In this case there need be no market disequilibrium implied. There may be no choice problem with regard to the complementarity of the two domains of investment or the distinction of the time horizons involved (as discussed in Section 2.4), or of the distinction between micro- and macroeconomic logic in investment decisions in education (as discussed in Section 2.5). But society may, nevertheless, see a dilemma of choice here because of the interpersonal comparisons involved. Social choice problems of this explicit kind occur in Examples 5 and 6 in Chapter 4 where unequal rewards for education and unequal opportunities for entry into school, respectively, are discussed.

The social-choice dilemmas encountered in the examples are classified in the following discussion according to whether they arise in the indirect way by *implication*, or in the direct way *explicitly*. To make a broad simplification, and putting it slightly differently, one may say that Type 1 problems of social choice can be seen in the context of the societal concern for economic efficiency (and, therefore, may be seen only indirectly as collective-choice problems), whereas Type 2 problems are best visualized in the context of societal concern for equity and social justice (and, therefore, visualized directly as collective-choice problems). Considerations of the Type 2 problems are only sometimes associated with, but can be quite independent of, considerations of disequilibrium or inefficiency in the market.

It may be calculated from the following references that there are *nine* different kinds of social-choice dilemmas in educational investments that are mentioned in the course of the analysis of the six examples in Chapter 4. Of these, one could place six in Type 1, and the remaining three in Type 2.

## 5.2 Type 1: Direct concern for efficiency

Of the six Type 1 dilemmas, four originate from domain-distinct considerations and are listed as $D_1$, $D_2$, $D_3$, and $D_4$. The remaining *two* are attributable to micro–macro considerations and are listed as $M_1$ and $M_2$.

### *$D_1$: Individual expectation versus labor needs*

The context of a potential dilemma was set in the Brazilian ma (Example 1), but it is easily conceivable that societal decision makers also would be guided in many other instances by what was perceived as the economy's future labor needs. Investments in the institutional domain, in that case, might be determined by that perception though individuals did not have a matching perception of the market's future needs for their services as trained labor. If there a divergence of this kind, naturally the needed investments in the individual domain would not be forthcoming and labor planning would fail.

The dilemma for social policy (either as fiscal policy or as policy determining the nature and extent of direct societal investment in education) might arise here from the following considerations. First, the societal perception of labor needs might have been based on plan needs and not on the anticipated demand of the market. Second, even if the needs were perceived on the basis of anticipated market demand at acceptable rates of earnings for trained personnel, the societal expectation and the individual expectation might still legitimately differ through a simple difference in objectives. For example, society might want in a given situation to insure against possible shortages of labor and would accept, in that situation, a quantum of unemployment of technical workers. Obviously, with the same expected demand, the societal investor would be induced to err on the side of extra capacity. On the other hand, individuals might want in that same situation to insure against possible unemployment and would invest cautiously in their own domain. It is obvious, perhaps, that the relative roles might well be reversed in other situations in which society might want to avoid unemployment, and individuals would want to take a calculated risk.

Given this situation, should social (perhaps fiscal) policy encourage individuals to alter allocations of funds in their domain and match the societal perception, or should it encourage institutional investors to alter allocations in their domain to match individual expectations?

### *$D_2$: Individual stratagem: brain drain*

Example 2 presents the following possible dilemma: Village-level workers might be investing in their bachelor of science degree in agriculture only to get out of the village forever! Obviously, the same problem might be latent in many other choice situations. Basically the ground for it is well laid whenever individuals are found to invest in a line of education for themselves exactly as required and provided for by investments in the institutional domain, but are suspected to do so for a purpose quite different from what societal policy had ever intended. There could be several valid reasons for this kind of contrary behavior or, more accurately, behavior that would prove to have been contrary in retrospect. Of the possible reasons, I shall briefly mention two fairly obvious ones.

In the first place, individuals might find it more profitable to invest in a particular line *X* than to go for their preferred training in *Y*, because (a) *X* was more attractively subsidized (through provision of more scholarships, better facilities, etc.), or (b) they felt that there was in some other way relative social approbation attached to the study of *X*, or simply because (c) *X* was the softer option, easier to score high marks in, for example, yet with the same kind of job opportunities as *Y*.

If there were a job available that did not bar graduates in *X* and also did not promise to make any use of the training in *X*, but that offered better prospects for persons interested in *Y*, then individuals might find it both easy and profitable to switch to a line in their careers for which, it might appear, they had never been prepared. In this way, some students could be found to be abandoning the areas in which they had been successfully trained (science, medicine, engineering) and taking up jobs as business executives, for example.

In the second place, individuals might have chosen exactly the training that they preferred and had an obvious aptitude for, but they might also intend to depart in due course with the acquired human capital for another more promising land.

In either case, there is a conflict in objectives between the individuals concerned and societal decision makers. But since the conflict does not surface until relatively late in the individuals' careers, there is very little that social policy (or more specifically, taxation policy) can do about it at the point of their entry into the line of training concerned. But what part should it play at later points in the individual's earning life? To be specific, the question for fiscal policy after the individuals have entered their chosen fields of occupation can be: To what extent should what is *presumed* to be in the social (even national) interest prevail over what is *revealed* to be the private interest of (a group of) individuals in determining the individuals' liability? To what extent should individuals be penalized for effecting a "strategic" entry into a line of education?[2]

### $D_3$: *Ambiguity of insufficient response*

We can see in virtually all the examples, but particularly in Examples 3, 4, and 6, the possibility of the target groups' not coming forward readily enough to invest sufficiently in the particular education and training that the institutional investors had provided for them. But the question that then often remains difficult to resolve is whether the reluctance of a particular group to invest in their education is a result of (a) their perception of a relatively bleak state of the market, (b) some curricular inappropriateness of the program, or even (c) some peculiar disadvantage faced by the group in the shape of, say, biased norms of performance. It may be mentioned that this last factor was precisely the one raised in Example 3, which dealt with the extent of participation of older women in regular college programs with young women, for effecting reentry into the work force.

The question, however, obviously has more general applicability and should be raised in all instances of special programs for the education of special groups. Besides the immediate problem of securing the supporting complementary investment in the individual domain, which is the problem of achieving an equilibrium of places provided and taken, there is also a social-choice problem here whose existence would be recognized once the basis for differentiating the special group from the rest of society was understood. But the exact nature of that problem will be illusive, because the dilemma here lies in deciding which answer to choose for the question of why the group did not participate, that is, invest, in their individual domain as much as required. The question of investing in educational facilities for such a group invariably will involve a comparison of such facilities with those available to competing groups, and here enter all the old questions of interpersonal comparability, equity, and social justice. A complicated collective-choice problem thus arises by implication even though the direct concern of the societal or institutional investor might be limited only to a certain possible disequilibrium between the facilities provided for the special group and the facilities utilized by it.

### *$D_4$: Long run, short run*

The choice problem involved in the time-horizon aspect of the domain-distinction argument was discussed at some length in the treatment of Example 1. But the same problem is present in the other examples, as well. Sometimes the societal investor can choose between a long-term investment in education, such as setting up a school, for example, and a relatively short-term project. The question that must be considered from the societal standpoint in this situation is principally that of the time horizon. But it is important to note that this question of time has to be considered in two distinct contexts.

First is the expected life span of the object of investment. If the prospective investment is in a school building, then that implies a fairly long life span. On the other hand, if the investment is intended to provide teaching material for running a training program, then that might imply a much shorter life span.

Second, there is, of course, the time perspective of the societal investor with respect to the actual individuals society is supposed to be investing for. How far into the future does one want to look? If that school building was for providing education to the young, and the project was for retraining older factory workers, then the former was long-term and the latter short-term in a second sense, too. A question before the societal decision maker, or for public finance policy, then is this. How many generations of individuals are involved in the calculations for the return to the investment in view? Seen in terms of social choice, setting priorities between long-term and short-term investments could thus turn out to be actually choosing between the conflicting objectives of persons who belonged to different generations, or even to different times.

### *$M_1$: Impact on returns*

The macroeconomic argument as used to examine the impact of investments in education on returns was introduced in Chapter 2 (Section 2.5). I have tried to apply it to Example 1, under *Macroeconomic considerations*. I rely upon a proposition whose plain economics is simple enough and would apply equally to the other examples: Individuals, in deciding on their own investments and calculating returns in terms of their lifetime earnings, are reasonably justified in viewing the ruling market rates of return to education as their guiding parameter, because the time span over which they have to assume their calculations would hold is comparatively short. On the other hand, societal investors have far less justification for assuming the parametric role of the rate of returns, because they must consider the impact of the aggregate of *all* investments in education on the market and they must think in terms of a much longer time span.

The implication of the proposition in terms of the possible disequilibrating effect of the widely different viewpoints of the micro- and macroinvestors in education is immediate. This leads, however, to the emergence of a basic social-choice problem as well. Assuming that education, at a given level, must be restricted – on the consideration, say, of the adverse impact of a larger aggregate investment on returns to education – to a smaller number than those who are *ready* to invest in it, how does society choose? Whatever society does would amount to choosing among different groups of individuals, thus reducing the situation to a basic social-choice dilemma.

### *$M_2$: Probability of employment*

The following simple but interesting result was discussed in Chapter 2 (Section 2.5). If, for each individual, the probability of securing employment is less than 1, then there exists the certainty of unemployment in the aggregate. The proposition reappears as the second macroeconomic consideration introduced in the analysis of Example 1 in Chapter 4. It may be recalled that the first macroeconomic consideration was of the impact of the aggregate investment in education on returns, which was taken up under the social-choice problem $M_1$ above.

The social-choice problem involved in the present case is straightforward enough: If each individual finds it profitable to take a calculated risk of unemployment while investing in education, and if society collectively prefers to avoid unemployment of trained individuals, then what could be the guiding principle for collective choice? I need not elaborate on this point here again except to note that the dilemma $M_2$ is similar to, but not quite the same as, the one I visualize as the social-choice dilemma $M_1$. In the latter case, while considering the impact of large increases in the aggregate investment in education, I implicitly assume that there is no doubt (in the minds of the individuals) either about the outcome (i.e., a sharp drop in rates of return) or about the outcome's unacceptability. Therefore, everybody presumably agrees that entry to the level of education concerned *has* to be restricted. The social-choice question, then, is who should have the right to buy advanced training with jobs to follow at higher rates of earnings? The question of "how many" is assumed here to have an agreed upon answer determined by the condition that the rate of earnings has to be maintained at an acceptable level.

In the $M_2$ case, on the other hand, the principal casualty of a large increase in the aggregate investment in education is presumed to be the employment prospect of the individuals being educated and not necessarily their rates of earnings, if employed. Therefore, individuals are assumed to be able to assess their own prospects on the basis of a given rate of earnings in a job in view following their education, as well as the probability of getting that job. Here the social-choice problem, then, arises a little differently from $M_1$. One might say that it arises one step earlier, and in the following form: Should everybody (and if not everybody, then *who*?) have the right to buy advanced training with only a probability of better jobs to follow?

## 5.3 Type 2: Direct concern for equity and social justice

Of the nine kinds of social-choice problems cited in Chapter 4, six have already been accounted for in the category Type 1 in the last section. The remaining three comprise the Type 2 problems. These are the dilemmas that arise when the social concern for equity and justice is direct, but society is at the same time faced with an ambiguity in interpreting, from the standpoint of equity and justice, some investment behavior of the individual. Three such ambiguous situations, which will be described, have been labeled $A_1$, $A_2$, and $A_3$. They constitute only a small sample in our collection because they arise only when social concern for equity is explicitly introduced. Type 2 problems would not need much elaboration because, being explicitly admitted social-choice problems, they do not depend on special interpretation. However, as the analysis of the Type 1 problems would have shown, it is still useful to be able to pinpoint the particular societal dilemma in each case. This is what I will try to do for the three Type 2 dilemmas. The situations in which the three kinds of dilemmas occur in the examples are briefly reexamined as follows.

### *$A_1$: Ambiguity of complex individuals*

As noted in Example 4, the success of the societal effort in programs for education for veterans in the United States depends on society's ability to take due note of the special susceptibilities of veterans.

However, this task is made more difficult sometimes by the subjects themselves, as in the case of black veterans, who suffer from a double trauma. This, I suggested, is not an isolated factor found only in the United States, but has its counterpart in many countries. When an individual is subject to multiple deprivations (being black and having had to fight in Vietnam, in this case), his sense of equity and social justice might well be revealed to be comparatively more complex and more difficult to satisfy than in the normal case of "single" deprivation. Perhaps this factor may be explained in terms of the "irrationality" of the individual or even a group of individuals who go through severely traumatic experiences.

But, on the other hand, this may well be one instance of a far more general phenomenon where the individual concerned would be found to be perfectly rational, only more complex than the fairly simple and "normal" rational person is usually assumed to be. Being more complex, the unusual rational person might hold on to more than one compatible set of preferences or judgments. He might respond to societal efforts to draw him out and give him a fair deal as a black veteran, as in our example, by acting in his individual domain sometimes as black and at other times as a Vietnam veteran. This implies that the character of his efforts to achieve equality (if any efforts *are* noticed), for example, would be more difficult to follow and match from the standpoint of the societal investor if that equality were a societal goal. In other words, it would be simpler for the societal investor in education, for example, to determine what to provide for him if he were only black or only a veteran. In having to choose for a group of "complex" individuals, therefore, society faces an additional choice problem between the different interests and judgments of the same individuals.

### *$A_2$: Ambiguity of unequal returns*

Consider the case where the same investment in schooling for two different groups of individuals brings in two different kinds of returns. The blacks and the whites in Example 5 are two such groups. They live in the same urban ghettos, go to the same schools, and presumably invest equally in their own education. Yet, blacks consistently get lower returns to investment in terms of the rates of earnings and are also more prone to unemployment. This is regarded in the context of the example as socially unacceptable, and one of the remedies suggested is *more* investment in special educational programs for blacks. If they are better educated and, therefore, better qualified for the same jobs whites apply for, then presumably discrimination against them would not operate to the extent of denying them the jobs.

It is necessary to note here the exact nature of the societal dilemma involved in considering this remedy (assuming, of course, that it would work). On the one hand, the market testifies that the marginal productivity of whites is higher and, therefore, more should be invested in their education. On the other hand, one's common sense (or conscience?) suggests that the lower rating of blacks is undeserved and, therefore, more should be invested in *their* education to redress the wrong. The social-choice dilemma here lies in the following ambiguity: How much of the inequality of returns is due to plain discrimination and how much to relative inefficiency?

It would seem that leaving out the extreme examples of discrimination (the example of the American urban ghettos could clearly be one), the social-choice problem involved in resolving the ambiguity of unequal rewards of education would be, by itself, of serious concern for social policy. The societal concern, however, is likely to be even greater, I may point out, because the criterion of equity, when it has to be explicitly defined, may not necessarily be made to imply equality of returns if discrimination is presumed but some relative inefficiency is not ruled out. How far society would go to restore the balance in favor of an admittedly disadvantaged group therefore remains an additional question of social choice.

### *$A_3$: Ambiguity of observed unequal participation*

Finally, there is another ambiguity that generates social-choice dilemmas in educational investment: the observed unequal participation of groups of individuals in the schooling system. Two instances of this, one in the United States and the other in France, were cited in Example 6, and the social-choice problems involved in the examples were discussed fairly extensively in the last chapter. I shall thus only briefly refer to them here, mainly to reiterate the general applicability of the argument in a wide variety of choice situations in education.

Social-choice problems associated with unequal participation in the schooling system can be of *two* kinds. First – and here the similarity with $A_2$ problems is obvious – are the kind of problems that would raise the following questions. Assuming that a group of individuals had not come forward and spent money and effort as readily as some other groups on a given educational program, had the individuals in the group stayed back from it because (a) the program did not suit their requirements as well as it suited the others' requirements; or (b) their entry into or stay in the program proved more difficult than for the others; or (c) they feared that the returns to education at the end of the program would prove to be lower for them than for the others; or (and this is a crucial source of ambiguity) (d) they were not sufficiently motivated or intellectually or otherwise equipped for the program?

It is interesting to note that a positive answer to each of these four questions may call for a different investment decision from society. For example, if the curriculum proved unsuitable for the group, then the remedy would possibly be investment in a different program for them. If the abilities of the individuals did not *match* those currently required for the program, then perhaps there should be some investment in special orientation courses. If it were feared that there would be discrimination at the end of the program with regard to employment, then as in the last case under $A_2$, the remedy suggested could be more investment in the education of the group to make discrimination against it more difficult to practice.

Finally, if the group did not seek further education because it did not care, or was not academically up to it, then society must consider whether the goal of equity implies equal participation in schooling. Each of the four different points of investment decision for society, it may be observed, requires a comparison of the interests and judgments of the group concerned (or, rather, of the individuals concerned) with those of the rest of society. This is the crux of the $A_3$ group of social-choice problems of the first kind.

Second, assume that regardless of the reasons that might lie behind an observed inequality in participation – these could be any from among the four suggested, or even others – the societal goal is equality. In that case, if the accepted criteria of inequality happen to be multiple, then social choice might face what economists would call an "index number problem." In the French case, for example, suppose that society seeks to establish equal educational opportunities for the children of town dwellers and children living in the rural cantons, *and* also between the children of workers (both industrial and agricultural) and children coming from the higher-income classes. Society may now have to solve the problem of assigning relative weights to the twin goals of equality: (a) between urban and rural children, and (b) between children from higher-income groups and working-class children. The social-choice dilemma may then be whether there should be more schools in the villages (which might help the rural rich) or more schools in the towns (which might benefit the urban poor)? Clearly, the probability of this kind of a dilemma arising in societal investment decisions increases rapidly with the number of ways in which the population is partitioned in the social perceptions of inequality – for example, between the sexes, classes, religions, castes and geographical and political regions.

## 5.4 The equity–efficiency quandary?

Finally, what implications will the two-way classification of the social-choice dilemmas have for one's understanding of the relationships that might exist between efficiency considerations and equity considerations?

Schultz, Bowles, Hansen, Johnson, and others speculated on precisely these relationships in the Schultz (1972) symposium on the equity–efficiency quandary in investment in education.[3] They did so, however, mainly on the basis of the evidence on, first, the effect of alternative policies of financing education (including policies on tuition charged) on individual optimizing investment decisions in education, and second, the effect of education itself on the distribution of personal income. It must be pointed out that the efficiency of individual investment decisions in education need not be thought of necessarily in terms of allocative efficiency alone. And similarly, equity in education need not necessarily be defined solely in terms of the effects on the distribution of income. But however efficiency of investment in education is viewed, and whichever way equity is defined, it is undoubtedly only at the level of factual information that the relation between efficiency and equity (both as defined) can be established.

In other words, an incompatibility between efficiency and equity – the so-called equity–efficiency quandary – need not be presupposed. Nevertheless, it is possible to come to a few general conclusions that seem to follow from the analysis offered in the preceding chapters, and from the classification of the social-choice dilemmas, whether or not these were actually drawn in the treatments of the individual examples. These conclusions might help to clarify, to a certain extent, the basis of the relationship between equity and efficiency in investments in education. To bring this discussion to a close, I present these conclusions, without further ado, as a set of propositions.

### *Not disjoint questions*

Our basic proposition is that efficiency and equity are *not* disjoint questions in educational investments. The two are related through the very two-domain characteristic of such investments that I have tried to bring out in this study. However, in the Type 1 social-choice situations, though a question of equity often will eventually arise, it will always do so indirectly. It may be recalled that the question surfaces *only* when there is some evidence of disequilibrium in the market in the sense that a lack of correspondence between educational investment in the institutional domain and in the individual domain is revealed. The mismatching of the two sets of investments can be brought about by forces that tend to inhibit (or overexcite) the necessary complementary investments by individuals to secure their education, corresponding to the institutional investments for providing it. This is the kind of lack of correspondence that can be anticipated by the considerations of the domain-distinction argument. On the other hand, the mismatching can similarly be brought about entirely by the workings of the microlevel logic of individual investments and the macrolevel logic of the aggregate investment in education. As we have seen, these need not be mutually compatible. If there is no breakdown at the level of either of the two sets of forces the equity–efficiency question simply may not be noted in Type 1 situations.

The equity–efficiency quandary may, however, quite legitimately be visualized directly in all the Type 2 social-choice situations, since there one will have a notion of what is equitable without reference to the optimization process and without waiting to see whether efficiency has broken down. But even with the presumption of direct societal concern for equity and social justice there is usually also an implied indirect concern for long-term efficient solutions. To put it another way, a social-choice dilemma between what is immediately efficient and what is immediately equitable is usually reducible to a social-choice dilemma between two solutions, each eventually efficient, though each would represent a contrary set of interests or judgments. In light of this comment, the three subsidiary propositions noted in the following discussion should provide the necessary limits to the equity–efficiency quandary, even in situations where its possible presence cannot reasonably be excluded.

### *Equity–efficiency in subsidies*

The first of these three propositions may be put in the context of subsidies to education that directly reduce the burden of individuals' investment in their own domain. The case for a subsidy to education can be justified up to a point for reasons of both efficiency and equity. For example, the argument of external productivity of education (which is a social-efficiency argument) will support subsidization. The argument that lower tuition for all students, for example, will make it easier for poor students to have access to education (which is an equity argument), will do likewise. The conclusion, therefore, is that in real life there may be an area of investment decisions in education over which both efficiency and equity considerations can point in the same direction.[4] The problem, it must be admitted, remains of demarcating the boundaries of that area.

### *High-quality personnel*

The next proposition arises from a consideration that should concern labor planners for high-quality personnel. In Chapter 1, while discussing the usefulness of the concept of unit cost of production of "quality outputs" such as first-rate physicists, I speculated on the effect of the group on the quality of the individual's education. To produce five good sports cars, I said, it would not be necessary to produce them in the company of fifteen others. But to produce five good physicists it might be essential to persevere with a class of twenty. To take a hypothetical example similar to the one used in Chapter 2, suppose there are twenty promising candidates for admission to a high-powered physics course, and only five anticipated positions for high-powered physicists at the end of the course. If society wishes for a reasonably high probability of getting five excellent physicists at the end of that course, then *all* twenty promising young people have to be taken through it. In that case, society does *not* have to face the social-choice problem of having to select five from among twenty equally promising people for admission to the course since admitting all twenty is found to be more efficient.

In other words, if the outcome of an investment in education cannot be viewed as certain, but can be stated probabilistically, then the requirement will be to start with a larger number of students than what is finally desired. The conclusion, therefore, is that in such circumstances the pursuit of efficiency itself might involve the pursuit of equity of a kind, from a societal point of view.

### *Long-term development*

Finally, there is always the long run. A probabilistic approach to the *development* of human resources *over time* would go far beyond the consideration of producing only top-quality personnel, which was the sole concern in the preceding example. Such an approach would legitimately encourage the advocates of the equity principle to hope that the wider the number base, at *any* given level of education, the greater the prospect of *eventually* being able to train the right people for the right jobs in all kinds of specialized employment associated with that level. The conclusion, therefore, is that equity today may mean efficiency tomorrow, and when it does, it would also mean a higher level of productivity of education tomorrow. Let me bring this section to an end on this highly optimistic note.

## 5.5 Economics of education and social policy: a concluding remark

I have argued throughout this study mainly for an explicit recognition of heterogeneity of structures in investment in education – heterogeneity in the types of human capital formation, in the domains of the decision making involved, in the kinds of the objectives set before the decision makers, and in the interests and the judgments of the decision makers. I have also tried to bring out some of the social-choice dilemmas that will be found to be intrinsic to such recognition of heterogeneous structures. In so doing I suggested, in effect, that a new economics of education was needed that must address itself explicitly to the various kinds of heterogeneity, breaking away from the comforting and composite paradigms of conventional approaches. This study has tried to indicate only the direction of the analysis to be undertaken and the dimensions of the questions involved. The task of providing a more constructive general theory remains, and it will not be an easy one. It will involve the application of social-choice theory in a way that it has not yet generally been applied. One still awaits the application of social-choice theory to macroeconomics as such and the resultant emergence of a new body of welfare economics. The emergence of a new welfare economics of *education*, in terms of social choice, may have to be impromptu, in a manner of speaking. A common set of questions may indeed be identified, as I have tried to do in this study. But subsequent discussion must be in terms of alternative collective-choice rules in the specific context of each choice situation in education, and in terms of the specific problems of interpersonal comparability and interpersonal value judgments involved. The answers, therefore, may come to us only piecemeal and individually tailored until their general patterns are recognized.

# Notes

## 1. Analogies of economics for economics of education

1 For one set of ideological objections to the concept of "human capital," see Bowles and Gintis (1975).

*Human capital* has been used throughout this study in the usual sense (as in Schultz 1960, Debeauvais 1962, Becker 1964, etc.) of enhanced productive power embodied in persons and brought about through learning. A more general concept is, of course, both possible and at times even likely to be more useful, particularly when one keeps in view some of the long-term objectives of institutional investments in education. Such a generalized concept would include in human capital at least one important *physical* component, namely, all the stored information necessary for maintaining and advancing the state of our learning. As David Attenborough (1979, p. 308) so dramatically puts it: "Today, our libraries, the descendants of those mud tablets, can be regarded as immense communal brains, memorising far more than any one human brain could hold. More than that, they can be seen as extracorporeal DNA, adjuncts to our genetical inheritance as important and influential in determining the way we behave as the chromosomes in our tissues are in determining the physical shape of our bodies."

2 The analogy of the firm for the individual investing in human capital is present throughout Schultz's treatment. For example, he assumes that, "the optimal investment in this form of human capital is basically dependent upon the microdecisions of students functioning as firms, and these are as efficient as any other large set of private firms" (Schultz, 1972, p. 22).

3 Perhaps it would be more accurate to suggest that what economists before Schultz (1960), or to be fair, before Mincer (1958), did not see was that individuals' allocation of expenditure on their education, like their other investments, could be carried out in expectation of returns measured in terms of the stream of costs incurred on behalf of, and the stream of earnings received from, the human capital (in themselves) over a lifetime. So far as the societal concern for skill formation is concerned, its importance has always been recognized in quite specific terms by economists. An obvious example would be Marshall (1927), particularly in his discussion on "The Aims of English Education Reform" (p. 208).

4 Presidential Address to the American Economic Association, 1960, reprinted as Schultz (1961).

5 For an extensive account of the measurements of rates of return on investment in education in various countries, see Psacharopoulos (1973).

6 I use *human capital* here and elsewhere in the same restricted sense as in Note 1.

7 Ben-Porath (1967, p. 364) hints at this aspect (which is different from that of normal aging or obsolescence) succinctly: "Not much has been said of $\delta$, the rate of deterioration. Consideration ought to be given to cases where $\delta$ is negative rather than positive as assumed here and also to the dependence of deterioration on the allocation of human capital to different activities."

Sen (1966) discusses the positive aspect of the aging process: the gain in experience or "learning by doing." This is related to, but different from, the aspect I emphasize here: the dependence of learning by doing on the *kind* of thing one is able to do.

8 See, for example, Ahmed (1975), p. 58.

9 I have made the simplifying assumption here and in the rest of the study that the individual student and the institutional teaching establishment are two different decision-making agencies. This will obviously leave out an interesting though presumably small class of individuals who would be self-taught and who, therefore, would be investors in both domains.

A more comprehensive analysis of the types of investors in the two domains is provided by Binod Khadria in his unpublished doctoral dissertation, *Determinants of Skill-Formation*, Jawaharlal Nehru University, New Delhi, 1982. Khadria points out that even institutions or governments invest in the individual domain when they subsidize individual expenses on buying education. Cross-investment also can take place in the other direction.

10 In what way, it may be asked, does this two-part account of the educational activity differ from the activity in a barbershop where the barber (like the teacher) obviously cannot perform unless the customer (the student) comes forward to get the haircut (the lesson)? It differs only to the extent that it is not taken as a description of the sale of a *service* to a consumer though education can indeed be so described. Here, however, the presumption is that what is being described is investment in education and this is to be counted as the total of what the provider of the service invests while giving it, and what the receiver of that service spends in obtaining it. (See also Chapter 2, Note 4.)

11 The last is, of course, only a particular application of the more general dictum that all social-choice questions in a democracy will eventually reduce to questions of collective choice.

12 The three arguments are elaborated in Chapter 2 as the domain-distinction argument (Section 2.4), the micro–macro argument (Section 2.5), and the collective-choice argument (Section 2.6), respectively.

13 No sensible economist would naturally try to sell the microeconomic production function analogy at this level of simplicity. But as we shall see later, the idea that this analogy is "illuminating" is sometimes put across and used in analysis.
14 Woodhall and Blaug (1965), p. 484.
15 Woodhall and Blaug (1965), section on "Some Conceptual Problems."
16 Woodhall and Blaug (1965), section on "Some Conceptual Problems."
17 I presume here that education as a process of "screening" requires a different paradigm from that of education as a process of "production." It may also be remarked that there can indeed be the case of a regular firm engaged in an unusual line of activity to which the production paradigm would be similarly inapplicable. One example could be that of a firm engaged in wildcat drilling for oil where the proportion of rejects is, by definition, bound to be high – perhaps even higher than in the education system's search for talent.
18 One complexity in the specification of the cost function in educational processes may be seen as of the following kind. In the case of physical production usually the quality is assumed given, and the quantity of the output $X$ stated as a function of the cost $C : X = f(C)$. In educational processes, on the other hand, the quality of the output is itself an important, additional, and incompletely specified, variable. It is in many cases presumed to vary directly with unit cost.
19 From the standpoint of labor planning needs this would imply that the principle of "safety in numbers" might prove important in fixing the targets of admission to courses in training for certain categories of high-quality personnel. Here the usual notion of wastage in terms of potentially unutilizable high-quality labor would not apply. This obviously has a bearing also on the relationship between efficiency and equity in investment in education, to be discussed in Chapter 5, under "The Equity–Efficiency Quandary."
20 By "technological" considerations I mean considerations such as, "How many graduate students should the professor have, given his range of academic interests and capabilities?" One can possibly think of a maximum and a minimum, perhaps occasionally even of a unique optimum in a given case, which will need no reference to relative prices at all. Unfortunately, however, such technical constraints are generally not known to determine decisions on student–teacher ratios.
21 See Woodhall and Blaug (1965), section on "An Index of Inputs."
22 It is at this point that the weakness of the parallel analogy, due to Schultz, of the student as the firm (see Note 2, this chapter) also shows up. Two distinguishing features of individuals' investment decisions for their own education make the process substantially different from the normal process of investment by a firm. First, since individuals here are themselves the raw material to be processed, the "rationality" of the decision maker involved is far more complex than what is comprehended in the economics of the firm. (For further comment see

Chapter 2, Note 9.) The second feature, discussed under the "domain-distinction argument," is that the individual's decision to *procure* education is dependent on the conditions governing the institutional decision to provide that education. The individual's entry into the "investment market" in education, therefore, is not free, like that of a normal firm. It is subject to the different admission requirements associated with the different opportunities that are partly determined by the institutional investor. For example, the information that engineering studies are much more profitable than humanities is irrelevant for the individuals who fail to meet the admission requirements of the engineering course.

23 For further comments see Note 7, Chapter 1 (Ben-Porath, 1967), Note 5, Chapter 2 (Schultz, 1967), Note 11, Chapter 2 (Stewart, 1975), Note 14, Chapter 3 (Rosen, 1972), and Note 15, Chapter 3 and Note 4, Chapter 5 (Johnson and Stafford, 1973).

## 2. Investment decisions in education

1 This, of course, would be subject to the fulfillment of the entry requirements referred to in Chapter 1, Note 22.

2 Strictly speaking, the more cumbrous "microeconomic logic vs. macroeconomic logic" argument would have been terminologically exact, since it indicates the possible contradiction between the microeconomic points of view of individuals and the macroeconomic considerations for the economy as a whole – both being relevant for arriving at societal judgments. Where only the macroeconomic considerations are implied, the more convenient "macroeconomic argument" will be used.

3 The distinction made here between individual "interests" and "judgments" is due to Sen (1977a). With regard to typical choice situations, Sen distinguishes between exercises of "interest aggregation" (wherein the personal interests of the individuals are aggregated) and exercises of "judgment aggregation" (wherein different persons' judgments about what is good for the community are aggregated). Sen (1979) also refers to "hybrid cases" in which the aggregation exercise takes into account both judgments and interests of the people involved, and he cites an example in Graaff (1977). In the case of educational investments, too, there will arise social-choice problems where both kinds of exercises are involved and where aggregate individual interests and aggregate individual judgments differ. As a hypothetical example presented in Section 2.5 will show, there could be a situation in which the aggregation of individual interests (of 100 science degree holders involved) signals that all interested students be trained further for a technical degree (with 81 jobs available at the end), whereas the aggregation of individual judgments of what is good for the economy *may* signal restricted entry to the technical course.

4 The distinction between individual and institutional investment decisions in education is frequently made in the literature, but seldom in the

sense of domain distinction as introduced here. For example, Lester Thurow (1970, see especially Chapters VI and VII) distinguishes clearly between investment decisions made by individuals, those made by firms for in-service training, and those made by the government. But what are not distinguished are the two domains of investment involved, facing each other in a characteristic configuration of giver and receiver in the process of education. The configuration does appear elsewhere, however, as supply and demand for the service of education (see, e.g., Correa, 1963, Chapters VII and VIII). I have already commented on the distinction of that approach from that of investment in education, in Chapter 1, Note 10.

5 Schultz (1967, p. 303) also mentioned the time-horizon aspect, though without distinguishing between the two domains (or the student and the school): "What is the relevant educational investment horizon in education? It is useful to distinguish between the *apparent behavioral horizons* of students and the *ex post horizons* underlying the estimates of rates of return. In thinking about the first of these – i.e., the investment horizon which will explain the behavior of students and schools – there are strong reasons for believing that it is, in general, fairly short. It is impossible to predict lifetime earnings; for the student to do so he would have to predict the changes in the demand for his type of education and the supply consequences of the decisions of others like himself to enter his particular field on his earnings up to 40 and more years ahead."

6 It may be asked whether individuals also may not invest in human capital for increasing the productive capacity of their own future generations. The answer to that, simply, is that even though they may *want* to, the returns on their education would be in terms of improving their own productive capacity and would be directly related only to their own earning profiles. However, if one used an extended definition of human capital that was less personalized (see, e.g., Chapter 1, Note 1), one could include investments in the individual domain that would earn returns over more than one generation through the accumulation of something like "family human capital."

7 The suggestion that the importance of the collective-choice argument becomes apparent when either the domain-distinction argument or the micro–macro argument fails to provide unambiguous signals for societal investment in education is elaborated on further in Section 2.6.

8 This curious jumbling of the microeconomic logic of individuals and the macroeconomic considerations for the economy as a whole is now standard practice in calculating the "refined" social rates of return to education. It has been resorted to, for example, in Blaug, Layard, and Woodhall (1969), Chapter 9, and commended also in Blaug (1970), pp. 227–8.

One interesting way of incorporating unemployment prospects in the analysis of individual investment decisions in education is explored in N. V. Varghese, *Manpower Planning in a Developing Economy: A Study in Education—Employment Linkages*, unpublished doctoral dissertation, Jawaharlal Nehru University, New Delhi, 1982. Varghese considers alternative education channels, each with its own probability of success, and each leading to a qualification linked to alternative job categories, with given probabilities of employment and given wages.

9 One may note, for example, the range and the variety of social-choice problems involved in the cases cited in Chapter 4.

10 For a discussion of multidimensional rationality, see Sen (1977b) and comments in Majumdar (1980).

11 As Frances Stewart (1975, p. 33) points out, social welfare can be assessed only after knowing the social objectives: "To select projects in such a way that net benefits are maximised is meaningless as a criterion of selection, until one has defined whose benefits one is talking about. Conflicts which arise depend on the extent to which different interests are differently affected by the projects being compared, and the extent to which the weighting of different classes does in fact differ."

12 The social-choice problem here is aggravated by the possibility that the external benefits of higher education are insignificant even to the extent of making the direct beneficiaries of the societal investment in the field almost the *sole* beneficiaries.

## 3. Rates-of-return tables in economics of education

1 For some rates of return calculated for individual countries see, in addition to Psacharopoulos (1973), Blaug (1968), Carnoy and Marenbach (1975), and Nallagounden (1967).

2 See Tables 3.1, 3.2, and 3.3 as the prototypes of the tables to be discussed. The tables have been renumbered, being Tables 3, 4, and 5 in Hansen (1963).

3 In other words, the rate of returns on human capital formation must be comparable definitionally to what Solow (1963, p. 34), for example, had postulated for physical capital formation: "Without any dubious 'measurement of capital' within whatever technological assumptions instinct and observation lead one to make, it is possible to pose and to answer what I have claimed to be the central question of capital theory. What is the payoff to society from an extra bit of saving transformed efficiently into capital formation?"

4 I refer mainly to what may be called "monopsonistic" exploitation of labor due to imperfections in the labor market.

5 See, for example, Balogh and Streeten (1963), Thias and Carnoy (1969), Bowles (1972).

6 See, for example, the Brazilian data in Fishlow (1975), pointed out by Bhaduri (1978), which distinguish income from work and income from property.

7 See Note 2, this chapter.
8 In some calculations these adjustments are introduced before making the estimation, as in Carnoy and Marenbach (1975). More usually they appear as adjustments to gross returns arrived at, as in Denison (1962) and Nallagounden (1967).
9 Hansen (1963), reprinted in Blaug (1968), p. 149.
10 Hansen (1963), reprinted in Blaug (1968), p. 149.
11 Blaug (1970), p. 226.
12 Blaug (1970), pp. 226–7.
13 *Margin* has been used in a curious variety of ways when describing investments in education. The confusion here is between the "investment of the marginal investor" and the "marginal investment of the average investor." It is, of course, to the latter that the rate of returns would relate in the normal usage of economics.
14 See Solow, quoted in Note 3, this chapter.
15 A similar idea is pursued by Rosen (1972, p. 341), who examines lifetime income and job choice as the basis of a model that suggests that it may be fruitful for some problems to view labor market contracts as essentially involving implicit forward contracts for future income. Sequential learning options, for example, are exercised by the maximizing individual implicitly through the job market showing preference for "jobs with a future."
16 A study by Johnson and Stafford (1973, p. 153), for example, found that the estimated marginal rates of returns to school quality were considerably higher than the corresponding rates of return to years of schooling. See also, Morgan and Sirageldin (1968). It must be pointed out, however, that the study by Johnson and Stafford also found that the marginal rate diminished for higher levels of quality (see Chapter 5, Note 4).

## 4. Social-choice problems in education

1 See Stoikov (1975), pp. 60–3.
2 See "Evaluation of Training in Brazil" (1966). *Training in Progress* 5, no. 4; p. 35.
3 This refers to a small-scale, but interesting and potentially important experiment in joining the formal with the nonformal in the Indian education system.
4 See Richard L. Shortlidge, Jr.: "University Training for *Gramsevaks* in India: An Example of Recurrent Education in a Low Income Country," reported in Stoikov (1975), p. 63.
5 The figures for the social rates of return as computed in the study are quoted here and accepted at their face value, but they call for a word of comment. Apart from the general problem of comparability of the rates of return to education, which was dealt with in the last chapter,

there seems to be an additional difficulty here. The social rate of return for the *gramsevaks*, whether calculated on the basis of their own promotion prospects or measured in terms of earnings of the regular graduates is, in either case, based on figures that relate to rates as administered by government and not as determined by the market. The fact that the civil service salaries of either the regular graduates or the trained *gramsevaks*, by and large, would not be subject to the forces of supply and demand makes the comparison of the two sets of rates less useful than the study apparently has assumed.

6 See Stoikov (1975), pp. 67–73.

7 See Wagner (1972).

8 See Caryl M. Kline, "Educational Planning for Mature Women," presented at the OECD Recurrent Education Conference, Washington, D.C., 1973, cited in Stoikov (1975).

9 See also Furth (1973).

10 See Stoikov (1975), pp. 72–8. Stoikov cites a series of articles appearing in the *International Labour Review*, between 1943 and 1947, describing programs in the United States, Great Britain, Canada, New Zealand, India, South Africa, and Australia.

11 See Cohen (1945).

12 See Stewart and Chambers (1950).

13 See H. and M. H. Peston (1973).

14 The reference is to Fendrich (1972). This could be construed as another example of the kind of multidimensional rationality referred to in Note 10, Chapter 2.

15 See Harrison (1972).

16 In this particular instance, "equal education" refers to "equal rewards for equal investments in education."

17 The U.S. example is taken from Schultz (1964). The French instance is from a comprehensive report by Pierre Laderrière (1967).

18 This is another instance where the value judgment against unequal participation (happily) persuades the economist to read the market signal in reverse: When a group of individuals is revealed to have cared less than other groups about the schooling of their children, it is presumed that there must be something wrong with the quality of the education available, and that more effort rather than less in providing better schooling to the children of the "reluctant" parents is indicated.

19 For further comments on the "quandary," see Section 5.4.

## 5. Social-choice dilemmas in education

1 The attempted classification is tentative, being based on the empirical characteristics of each choice problem encountered. However, the richness and variety of these characteristics suggest scope for further theoretical classification in terms of what Sen (1979, p. 113) calls the "appropriate

specification of the social choice format." This would mean classification either according to structures of the social-choice rules admitted (thus specifying the types of social welfare functions, or social-choice functions or other rules to be used), or according to axioms admitted within given structures (thus specifying the nature of the relationship assumed within the individual's set of alternatives – whether the independence condition is used; the nature of the relationship assumed between the utility functions of different individuals – whether and to what extent interpersonal comparability is assumed; and so on).

2 This could be described as plain deception by the individual provided, of course, no opprobrium was attached to such description, as there is no a priori case for placing the social interest above the individuals' private interests.

3 The title of this section is borrowed from that of the Schultz (1972) symposium, but with the question mark supplied. The possible conflicts between economic efficiency and equity, as I later suggest, are not necessarily unavoidable. A *desirable* solution (differentially subsidized tuitions, say), sometimes promises to be eventually efficient, though not immediately so, for the purposes of resource allocation. However, the so-called equity–efficiency quandary is often associated, and sometimes confused, with a deeper dilemma in education between the pursuit of equality and the pursuit of excellence. This section – indeed, the economics of education as such – has very little comment to offer on that more intractable problem lying at the heart of the social philosophy of education.

4 Johnson and Stafford (1973, p. 153) find evidence that quality influences earning, but the marginal effect of quality diminishes, so that, as they observe, "If our finding of diminishing marginal returns to school quality holds for students of different given abilities, then one implication is that equality and efficiency goals are not necessarily inconsistent." This evidence provides a somewhat different basis for the same conclusion.

# References


Ahmed, Manzoor (1975). *The Economics of Nonformal Education*. New York: Praeger.

Arrow, K. J. (1973). "Higher Education as a Filter," *Journal of Public Economics* 2: pp. 193–216.

Attenborough, David (1979). *Life on Earth*. Glasgow: Collins.

Balogh, T., and Streeten, P. P. (1963). "The Coefficient of Ignorance." *Bulletin of Oxford University Institute of Statistics* 25, no. 2: pp. 97–107.

Becker, Garry S. (1964). *Human Capital*. Princeton: Princeton University Press.

Ben-Porath, Yoram (1967). "The Production of Human Capital and the Life Cycle of Earnings," *Journal of Political Economy* 75, no. 4 (August): pp. 352–65.

Bhaduri, Amit (1978). "Education and the Distribution of Personal Income: An Analysis of Issues and Policies." *Industry and Development*, United Nations, no. 2, pp. 3–14.

Blaug, Mark, ed. (1968). *Economics of Education* 1. New York: Penguin Books.

ed. (1969). *Economics of Education* 2. New York: Penguin Books.

(1970). *An Introduction to the Economics of Education*. New York: Penguin Books.

(1974). *Education and the Employment Problem in Developing Countries*. Geneva: ILO.

Blaug, Mark, Layard, R., and Woodhall, M. (1969). *The Causes of Graduate Unemployment in India*. London: Lane.

Bowles, S. (1972). "Schooling and Inequality from Generation to Generation." *Journal of Political Economy* 80, no. 3 (supp. May/June): pp. 219–51.

Bowles, S., and Gintis, H. (1975). "The Problem with Human Capital: A Marxian Critique." *American Economic Review* 65, no. 2 (May): pp. 74–82.

Carnoy, M., and Marenbach, O. (1975). "The Return to Schooling in the U.S., 1939–69." *Journal of Human Resources* 10, no. 3 (Summer): pp. 312–32.

Chaudhri, D. P. (1977). *Education, Innovations and Agricultural Development: A Study of North India (1961–72)*. Armidale: University of New England.

Cohen, Wilbert J. (1945). "The Federal Government's Program for Ex-servicemen." *Annals of the American Academy of Political and Social Sciences* (Philadelphia), March: pp. 63–70.

Correa, Hector (1963). *The Economics of Human Resources*. Amsterdam: North-Holland.

Debeauvais, M. (1962). "The Concept of Human Capital." *International Social Science Journal* 14, no. 4, pp. 660–76.

Denison, E. F. (1962). *The Sources of Economic Growth in the United States and the Alternatives before Us*. New York: Committee for Economic Development.

Fendrich, James M. (1972). "The Returning Black Vietnam-era Veteran." *Social Service Review* 46 (March): pp. 60–75.

Fishlow, Albert (1975). "Income Distribution and Human Capital: Some Further Results for Brazil." In M. Parkin and A. R. Nobay, eds., *Contemporary Issues in Economics*, pp. 354–75. Manchester: Manchester University Press.

Furth, Dorothea (1973). "Issues in Short-cycle Higher Education." *Higher Education* 2, no. 1, pp. 95–102.

Graaff, J. de V. (1977). "Equity and Efficiency as Components of the General Welfare." *South African Journal of Economics* 45, no. 4, pp. 362–75.

Hallak, J. (1969). *The Analysis of Educational Costs and Expenditure*. Paris: UNESCO, International Institute for Educational Planning.

Hansen, W. Lee (1963). "Total and Private Return to Investment in Schooling." *Journal of Political Economy* 81, no. 2, pp. 128–40.

ed. (1970). *Education, Income and Human Capital*. Studies in Income and Wealth 35. New York: Columbia University Press.

Harrison, Bennett (1972). "Education and Unemployment in the Urban Ghetto." *American Economic Review* 62, no. 5 (December): pp. 796–12.

Jenny, Hans H. (1968). "Pricing and Optimum Size in a Nonprofit Institution: The University." *American Economic Review* 58, no. 2 (May): pp. 270–83.

Johnson, George E., and Stafford, Frank P. (1973). "Social Returns to Quantity and Quality of Schooling." *Journal of Human Resources* 8, no. 2 (Spring): pp. 139–55.

Johnson, H. G. (1972). "The Alternatives before Us." *Journal of Political Economy* 80, no. 3, (supp. May/June): pp. 280–9.

Laderrière, Pierre (1967). "Regional Inequalities of Opportunity in French Education and the Measures Designed to Reduce Them." In *Social Objectives in Educational Planning*, pp. 253–85. Paris: OECD.

Majumdar, T. (1980). "The Rationality of Changing Choice." *Analyse & Kritik* 2, Heft 2, pp. 172–8.

Marshall, Alfred (1927). *Principles of Economics* (8th edition). London: Macmillan Press.

Michelson, S. (1969). "Rational Income Decisions of Negroes and Everybody Else." *Industrial and Labor Relations Review* 23 (October): pp. 15–28.

Mincer, J. (1958). "Investment in Human Capital and Personal Income Distribution." *Journal of Political Economy* 66, no. 4 (August): pp. 281–302.

Morgan, James, and Sirageldin, I. (1968). "A Note on the Quality Dimension in Education." *Journal of Political Economy* 76 (Sept./Oct.): pp. 1069–77.

Nallagounden, A. M. (1967). "Investment in Education in India." *Journal of Human Resources* 2, no. 3 (Summer): pp. 347–58.

Peston, H., and M. H. (1973): "The Further Education and Training Scheme." Paper presented at the OECD Recurrent Education Conference, Washington, D.C.

Psacharopoulos, George (1973). *Returns to Education: An International Comparison*. Amsterdam: Elsevier.

Renshaw, Edward F. (1960). "Estimating the Returns to Education." *Review of Economics and Statistics* 42: pp. 318–24.

Ribich, T. I. (1968). *Education and Poverty*. Washington, D.C.: The Brookings Institution.

Rosen, Sherwin (1972). "Learning and Experience in the Labor Market." *Journal of Human Resources* 7, no. 3 (Summer): pp. 326–42.

Schultz, T. W. (1960). Presidential Address Before the American Economic Association, reprinted as Schultz (1961).

(1961). "Investment in Human Capital." *American Economic Review* 51: pp. 1–17.

(1962). "Reflections on Investment in Man." *Journal of Political Economy* 70 (supp.: Oct.): pp. 1–8.

(1964). "Underinvestment in the Quality of Schooling: The Rural Farm Areas." In *Increasing Understanding of Public Problems and Policies. 1964*: pp. 12–34. Chicago: Farm Foundation.

(1967). "The Rate of Return in Allocating Investment Resources to Education." *Journal of Human Resources* 2, no. 3 (Summer): pp. 293–309.

ed. (1972). *Investment in Education: The Equity-Efficiency Quandary*. *Journal of Political Economy* 80, no. 3 (supp.: May/June):s2–30.

Sen, A. K. (1966). "Education Vintage and Learning by Doing." *Journal of Human Resources* 1, no. 2 (Fall): pp. 3–21.

(1970). *Collective Choice and Social Welfare*. San Francisco: Holden-Day.

(1977a). "Social Choice Theory: A Re-examination." *Econometrica* 45, no. 1 (January): pp. 53–89.

(1977b). "Rational Fools: A Critique of the Behavioral Foundations of Economic Theory." *Philosophy and Public Affairs* 6: pp. 317–44.

(1981). "Social Choice Theory." In K. J. Arrow and M. *Intriligator*, eds., *Handbook of Mathematical Economics*. Amsterdam: North-Holland.

Solow, Robert M. (1963). *Capital Theory and the Rate of Return*. Amsterdam: North-Holland.

Stewart, Donald D., and Chambers, Richard P. (1950). "The Status Background of the Veteran College Student." *Sociology and Social Research* 35, no. 1 (September/October): pp. 12–21.

Stewart, Frances (1975). "A Note on Social Cost-Benefit Analysis and Class Conflict in LDCs." *World Development* 3, no. 1 (January): pp. 31–9.

Stoikov, Vladimir (1975). *The Economics of Recurrent Education and Training*. Geneva: ILO.
Thias, H., and Carnoy, M. (1969). *Cost Benefit Analysis of Education: A Case Study of Kenya*. Washington, D.C.: World Bank.
Thurow, Lester (1970). *Investment in Human Capital*. Belmont, Calif.: Wadsworth.
Vaizey, John (1962). *The Economics of Education*. London: Faber.
Wagner, Leslie (1972). "The Economics of the Open University." *Higher Education* 1, no. 2 (May): pp. 159–83.
Weisbrod, Burton A. (1964). *External Benefits of Public Education*. Princeton: Princeton University Press.
Woodhall, Maureen (1970). *Cost-Benefit Analysis in Educational Planning*. Paris: UNESCO, International Institute for Educational Planning.
Woodhall, M., and Blaug, M. (1965). "Productivity Trends in British University Education 1938–62." *Minerva* 3: pp. 483–98.
(1968). "Productivity Trends in British Secondary Education 1950–1967." *Sociology of Education* 41: pp. 1–35.

# Index